The New York Coffee Guide.

2020

Edited by
Jeffrey Young

Author: Allegra Strategies
Reviewers: Sally Paton, Daniel Powers, Stacey Grant, Richard Ehrlich, Marisa Kanter and Jeremy Hersh
Project Executive: Hannah Hill
Research: Corinne Smallwood, Maggie Cadden and John Imhoff
Photography: Ben Hider, Chérmelle D. Edwards, Sam & Melissa Ortiz and provided by venues
Design: John Osborne
Website: Tim Spring
Publisher: Allegra Publications Ltd

Visit our website:
www.newyorkcoffeeguide.com

@newyorkcoffeeguide

All information was accurate at time of going to press.

Published by Allegra Publications Ltd © 2019

Serendipity House, 106 Arlington Road, London, NW1 7HP, UK.

Foreword

by **Gavin Compton**, Owner, Variety Coffee Roasters

In 2008, I opened the first Variety Coffee. There were no bagels, no paninis, no salads - we just did coffee, a unique concept at the time. What we lacked in food offering we made up for in service. Our baristas' drive and determination made our operation work.

I can't think of a better time to have joined what would soon become New York's Third Wave scene. In 2010, Oliver Strand wrote 'the article' for The New York Times. It acted as the first comprehensive guide to specialty coffee in New York. Ten years on and the guide to coffee in NYC has expanded from Strand's 40 spots, peppered throughout the city, to a staggering 220 craft coffee venues. Every nook and cranny of New York's boroughs seems to host an artisan.

Looking back on the last decade, the role of the barista has grown alongside the coffee scene, blossoming from an entry-level service gig to a tangible and aspirational career path. Many baristas of those formative Third Wave years have gone on to shape and lead the wider industry today. They became roasters, green buyers, educators, cafe owners, influencers; it is because of the baristas that the Third Wave coffee movement was able to explode like it has.
The ensuing changes to landscape and product are clear - corner cafes have become chains, independent brands are being swept up by international conglomerates, and cold brew, the once most niche of the niche, a brew method for coffee zealots, is now the household term for cold coffee.

Despite these broader 5th Wave developments, New York coffee culture, at its core, continues to be defined by the baristas who have made its counters and cafes their homes. They are the ones pushing boundaries, the ones who pass on the passion for this product and industry. They wake up every day and ride empty trains to work because they love what they do, and their commitment sets an example for the rest of us.
The barista is the true driving force of our industry.

Contents

Introduction

Welcome to The New York Coffee Guide 2020 - the definitive guide to New York's best craft coffee venues.

Year on year, we endeavour to bring you the crème de la crème of New York's leading specialty coffee shops, cafes and roasteries. We're here to spill the (coffee) beans on all the latest and greatest places to get that all-important coffee boost. Whether you're searching for a morning flat white, a lunchtime long black, or an evening espresso martini, we've got plenty of top notch recommendations to keep you caffeinated.

With 28 new venues added to this 2020 edition, we now feature a total of 220 profiles in the guide. Look out for our 'New and Noteworthy' profiles dotted throughout the guide - these are venues we believe are exciting, must-visit additions to New York's flourishing specialty coffee scene.

The 5th Wave of coffee has become well and truly established in New York, with independent specialists adopting a boutique-at-scale approach to coffee and opening multiple sites with their winning recipe for success, whilst still retaining their unique character and high quality.

Allegra Strategies is an established leader in research and business intelligence for the coffee industry. We have drawn on this research as well as a variety of other sources to compile The New York Coffee Guide. We hope you enjoy it!

Photo: Seven Grams Caffé (Flatiron)

About the Guide

Every venue featured in The New York Coffee Guide 2020 has been visited by our expert team. We have two levels of ranking within the guide, both highlighted with a stamp: Top 40, and Top 10. The Top 40 are the venues that we feel bring something special to the coffee scene and are truly standout destinations for great coffee.
The Top 10 are superstar venues that are an absolute must-visit. Customer and industry feedback also inform the venue shortlist and the Top 40 & Top 10.

Key to symbols

In-store roastery 

Alternative brew methods available 

Decaffeinated coffee available 

Coffee beans sold on site 

Gluten-free products available 

Venue has a loyalty card 

Milk alternatives available 

Restrooms 

Parent & baby friendly 

Disabled access

Credit cards accepted

WiFi available

Alcohol served

Coffee courses available

Outdoor seating

Brunch available at weekends

Cold brew available 

Computer friendly 

Venues marked as 

are new to this edition of the Guide.

Venues marked as 

are venues added to this edition of the Guide that we feel are worthy of special mention.

Photo: Relationships NYC

A Brief History of New York Coffee Shops

THE EARLY YEARS

800 AD The coffee plant (Coffea) attracts human interest and consumption as early as 800 AD in the Kaffe region of Ethiopia. According to legend, it was an Ethiopian goat herder named Kaldi who first discovered how animated his herd of goats became after chewing on the red berries.

13TH - 16TH CENTURIES

Coffee berries are brought to the Arabian Peninsula and the first known cultivation of coffee is established in the area known today as Yemen. A crude version of coffee - roasted beans crushed and boiled in water - is developed and by 1475 coffee houses are established in Constantinople, Cairo and throughout Persia.

17TH AND 18TH CENTURIES

Travelers to the Arabian Peninsula bring coffee to Europe and Britain. Coffee houses are established as centers for the exchange of ideas and information, as well as forums for debate.

1650 The first English coffee house is established in Oxford by a Jewish gentleman named Jacob at the Angel in the parish of St Peter.

1668 Coffee is brought to New Amsterdam (Old New York) by Dutch settlers.

1696 Built in the style of the coffee houses of Europe, The King's Arms is the first coffee house established in New York.

1732 The Exchange Coffee House is opened on Broadway and establishes itself as a center for commerce.

1750 The Exchange Coffee House loses favor and is replaced by The Merchants Coffee House (on what is now known as Wall Street), which grows to be the foremost gathering place in the city for trade and political debate.

1765 A warning to the citizens of New York to end their rioting against the Stamp Act is read at The Merchants Coffee House.

1773 The Boston Tea Party, a revolt against the high taxation levied by King George III on tea imported to the New World, sees coffee replace tea as the drink of choice in the colonies.

1784 The Bank of New York, the oldest bank in the country, is founded at The Merchants Coffee House.

1792 The New York Stock Exchange is established at the Tontine Coffee House on Wall Street, where the first public stocks are sold.

19TH AND 20TH CENTURIES

With the rise of industrialization and technological advances, coffee drinking becomes accessible to everyone, not just the elite. People begin drinking it more in their homes and the demand for the beans rises, leading to rapid growth in coffee production.

1840 The Gillies Coffee Company is founded in New York, a company that survives as the oldest coffee merchant in the city.

1850 Folgers Coffee is founded in San Francisco.

1864 The first commercial coffee roasting machine, New York's Jabez Burns' #1 Coffee Roaster, receives a US patent.

1882 The Coffee Exchange of New York begins regulating the coffee trade, setting standards for the traffic of the commodity as well as the quality of the product.

1892 Maxwell House Coffee is founded.

1907 Porto Rico Importing Company opens on Bleecker Street.

1911 The National Coffee Association of the USA is established, the first trade association for the US coffee industry.

1920s As Prohibition takes effect, national coffee sales flourish.

1923 Green Coffee Association of New York founded.

1927 Caffe Reggio opens in Greenwich Village with the first espresso machine in New York.

1946 Coffee consumption in the US hits an all-time high, reaching 19.8 pounds per person per annum, twice what it was in 1900.

1950s / 1960s After WWII, the importation of coffee is impeded. The Pan American Coffee Bureau is established to promote the drinking of coffee and assist its production in Central America. One such promotion is the popularization of the 'coffee break'.

Italian-style cafes serving espresso and pastries begin to pop up in Greenwich Village and Little Italy. These coffee shops become creative and intellectual centers for artists, writers, musicians, and intellectuals.

1953 Howard Schultz is born in Brooklyn.

1971 Starbucks opens its first store at Pike Place Market in Seattle, Washington.

1982 The Specialty Coffee Association of America (SCAA) is founded.

Late 1980s

After an inspiring visit to Italy, Howard Schultz buys Starbucks and revamps the brand.

1994 Manhattan's first Starbucks store opens on the Upper West Side at 86th Street and Broadway.

1995 Intelligentsia Coffee & Tea opens in Chicago.

1999 Stumptown Coffee Roasters opens in Portland, Oregon.

The Cup of Excellence is established.

LAST DECADE

The 2000s see specialty coffee and the third-wave coffee movement emerge in the US, starting in Portland and Seattle and spreading to California, New York and beyond. This movement focuses on ethical trading, coffee freshness and new roasting techniques.

2000 The first World Barista Championship takes place in Monte Carlo.

2001 Ninth Street Espresso opens in Alphabet City.

2003 Gorilla Coffee opens in Park Slope, Brooklyn.

The first Joe location opened.

2005 Café Grumpy established.

2007 La Colombe Torrefaction opens its first New York outpost in Tribeca.

2009 Stumptown Coffee opens its first New York location at The Ace Hotel in Brooklyn.

2010 The Blue Bottle Coffee Company opens its roastery in a converted warehouse in Williamsburg, Brooklyn.

American Michael Phillips wins the World Barista Championship.

2012 The US Barista champion is Katie Carguilo.

Australian-owned Toby's Estate opens in Williamsburg, Brooklyn.

The New York Coffee Guide first published.

2013 The US Barista Champion is Pete Licata.

Key openings in the New York coffee scene include Devoción, Rex and Stumptown on West 8th Street.

2014 The US Barista Champion is Laila Ghambari.

Starbucks opens its first reserve store in Williamsburg.

2015 New York Coffee Festival launched.

The US Barista Champion is Charles Babinski.

Bluestone Lane on East 90th Street open their first store inside a church.

2016 The US Barista Champion is Lemuel Butler.

Taylor St. Baristas open their first New York store after their huge success in London.

2017 The US Barista Champion is Kyle Ramage.

New York Coffee Festival returns for its third year.

Variety open their first Manhattan outpost in Chelsea.

2018 The US Barista Champion is Cole McBride.

Starbucks Reserve opens its New York roastery in the Meatpacking District.

Devoción open their second Brooklyn venue.

2019 The US Barista Champion is Sam Spillman.

Devoción open their first Manhattan location in Flatiron District.

Stumptown Coffee Roasters open their first Brooklyn cafe, taking up residence in an 1860s firehouse in Cobble Hill.

Venue List

Lower Manhattan

East Village & Lower East Side

Soho & Neighboring

West Village & Neighboring

Chelsea

Midtown & Gramercy

* NEW ◊ TOP 40 ◊ TOP 10

Upper Manhattan

Park Slope & Surrounding

Downtown Brooklyn

Bushwick & Surrounding

Williamsburg

Greenpoint & Queens

Photo: Kinship Coffee

Lower Manhattan

East Village & Lower East Side

Soho & Neighboring

West Village & Neighboring

Chelsea

Midtown & Gramercy

119 PROOF Coffee Roasters (Carmel) p131
120 Ramini Espresso Bar p132
121 REMI Flower & Coffee p133 *
122 REX p134
123 Ruby's (Murray Hill) p134
124 Seven Grams Caffé (Flatiron) p135 *
125 Simon Sips p136
126 St Kilda Coffee p136
127 Stumptown Coffee Roasters (Ace Hotel) p137
128 Taylor St. Baristas p138 ◊
129 Think Coffee (Gramercy) p139
130 Trademark Taste + Grind p139
131 Wattle Cafe p140
132 Zibetto Espresso Bar p141 *
Central Park
N
Theater District / Times Square
Chelsea
Midtown & Gramercy
West Village & Neighboring
Gramercy Park
Hudson River
East River
Washington Square Park
Soho & Neighboring
East Village
Tribeca
Chinatown
East Village & Lower East Side
Lower East Side
Lower Manhattan
Brooklyn Bridge
Manhattan Bridge
FDR Drive
* NEW
◊ TOP 40
◊ TOP 10
1000 ft
2000 ft

Photo: Tyler Nix

Lower Manhattan is a diverse and exciting area with a variety of identities. The business-savvy Financial District has the hustle and bustle of Wall Street at its heart, while trendy Tribeca is a hip neighborhood that overlooks the Hudson River. By night, the Meatpacking District is immensely fashionable, with great shopping, chic restaurants and popular bars and clubs. Most importantly it is home to The World Trade Center.

Lower Manhattan

Black Fox Coffee Co

70 Pine Street, Manhattan, NY 10005 | **Financial District**

Black Fox is a beautiful downtown venue, located just around the corner from the South Street Seaport. The space is large and open, designed purposely to emphasize service and make everyone feel at one with the space. The owner makes it clear that he does not want to dictate taste, instead offering a small selection of high quality roasters to provide an element of choice. The menu is Australian inspired, with fresh ingredients prepared by a chef straight from Melbourne. Be sure to try the Australian take on the PB&J - you won't regret it.

www.blackfoxcoffee.com
Subway 2, 3 (Wall St)

MON-FRI. 6:30am - 5:30pm
SAT-SUN. 8:00am - 4:00pm

First opened 2016
Roaster Multiple roasters
Machine Kees van der Westen Spirit, 3 groups
Grinder Nuova Simonelli Mythos One, Mahlkönig EK 43, Mazzer Luigi Kold

Espresso	$3.75
Cappuccino	$4.50
Latte	$5.00

Bluestone Lane Financial District

90 Water Street, Manhattan, NY 10005 | **Financial District**

Photo: Ben Hider

Situated blocks away from South Street Seaport, Bluestone Lane's downtown venue might just be its cutest spot yet. It is not the largest of locations. However, what it lacks in square footage, it certainly makes up for in beauty - exposed brick and quartz counter tops add a premium touch to this venue. Bluestone Lane beans always hit the spot, and the full brunch menu is offered. Seating is limited, but it is also a perfect place to drop in for a flat white on your way to work.

(718) 374-6858
bluestonelane.com
Subway 2, 3 (Wall St)

Sister locations Multiple locations

MON-FRI.	7:00am - 5:00pm
SAT-SUN.	7:30am - 4:00pm

First opened 2016
Roaster Bluestone Lane
Machine La Marzocco Linea, 3 groups
Grinder Mazzer Luigi Robur E

Espresso	$3.20
Cappuccino	$4.25
Latte	$4.25

No. 2

Café Grumpy Financial District

20 Stone Street, Manhattan, NY 10004 | **Financial District**

Upon entering this Café Grumpy location, the visual experience is stunning. With beautiful artwork that adorns every wall, this cafe is reminiscent of a museum. As always, do not let the venue's name fool you - Café Grumpy baristas are among the most friendly and attentive in the city. As for the coffee, the Synesso pulls excellent shots from their specialty beans. Inserting itself in the ever-busy financial district, Café Grumpy is the perfect spot to take a break, slow down, and relax in the midst of your chaotic work day.

(646) 838-9306
cafegrumpy.com
Subway 4, 5 (Bowling Green) or R, W (Whitehall St)

MON-FRI. 6:00am - 7:30pm
SAT-SUN. 8:00am - 4:00pm

First opened 2017
Roaster Café Grumpy
Machine Synesso MVP Hydra, 3 groups
Grinder Nuova Simonelli Mythos One Clima Pro, Mahlkönig Guatemala

Espresso $3.75
Cappuccino $4.50
Latte $5.00

Sister locations Multiple locations

No. 3

Gotan

130 Franklin Street, Manhattan, NY 10013 | **Tribeca**

A spacious cafe full of blonde wood and huge windows letting in light, Gotan is a favorite among the well-dressed residents of Tribeca, and those who work in the area. The uniformed and bow-tied baristas are serious about their coffee, made on the fairly unique and handsome Modbar espresso machine, built right into the bar. Drop in for an expertly made latte - it is worth the trip.

(212) 431-5200
www.gotannyc.com
Subway 1, 2 (Franklin St)

Sister locations Midtown / Chelsea / Williamsburg

MON-FRI. 7:00am - 5:00pm
SAT-SUN. 8:00am - 5:00pm

First opened 2014
Roaster Counter Culture Coffee
Machine Modbar, 2 groups, La Marzocco
Grinder Nuova Simonelli Mythos One

Espresso	$3.50
Cappuccino	$4.25
Latte	$4.75

No. 4

Hole in the Wall Financial District

15 Cliff Street, Manhattan, NY 10038 | **Financial District**

Wedged between the narrow streets and towering office buildings of the Financial District, this lively Aussie-owned cafe has your AM and PM covered. By day it's all sun-drenched interiors buzzing with upbeat tunes and lively chatter, welcoming you in through an outdoor oasis of lush plants to enjoy light, earthy batch brews and expert flat whites teamed with healthy, hearty brunch fare. At 6pm the cafe transforms into the cracking bar and restaurant, Sugar Momma. Hold the espresso and take a martini instead.

(212) 602-9991
www.holeinthewallnyc.com
Subway 2, 3, J, Z (Fulton St)

Sister locations Murray Hill

MON-SUN. 7:00am - 5:00pm

First opened 2017
Roaster Novo Coffee
Machine Synesso MVP Hydra, 2 groups
Grinder Mazzer Luigi Robur E

Espresso	$3.25
Cappuccino	$4.25
Latte	$4.75

No. 5

Irving Farm New York Fulton Center

200 Broadway, Manhattan, NY 10038 | **Financial District**

While most of Irving Farm's early venues are very much 'Old New York', this location is all about new, new, new. Plunked down in the heart of the Fulton Center transit hub, it is inevitably a place where commuters abound. But it's also a good place to sit and watch the world go by, and to marvel at the shifting patterns of light cast down by the 'sky-reflector net' in the building's skylight. Irving's coffee is outstanding, whether pour over or espresso-based, and the latte art is a thing of true beauty.

(212) 206-0707
irvingfarm.com
Subway 4, 5, A, C, J, Z (Fulton St) or R (Cortlandt St)

MON-FRI. 7:00am - 7:00pm
SAT-SUN. 9:00am - 6:00pm

First opened 2016
Roaster Irving Farm New York
Machine La Marzocco Linea, 2 groups
Grinder Nuova Simonelli Mythos Clima Pro

Espresso $3.25
Cappuccino $4.50
Latte $4.75

Sister locations Multiple locations

No. 6

Joe Coffee Company World Trade Center

185 Greenwich Street, Manhattan, NY 10007 | **Financial District**

On a first visit to this branch of Joe, in the Westfield World Trade Center (also known as the Oculus), you may find yourself getting lost and asking for directions. Stick with it: this is a calm haven of good coffee in a shopping/transportation hub that's pretty much always packed. The look is bright and slightly space-age modern, and if you're not rushing off for work or taking a PATH train home, the seating is comfortable. Milky drinks are well presented, but drip brews (including decaf) are an equally big draw. As for the service, it couldn't be more friendly or efficient. Great job Joe!

joecoffeecompany.com
Subway 4, 5, A, C, J, Z, R (Fulton St) or E (World Trade Center)

MON-FRI. 6:30am - 6:00pm
SAT-SUN. 10:00am - 6:00pm

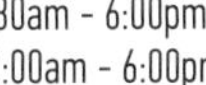

First opened 2017
Roaster Joe Coffee Company
Machine La Marzocco Linea PB, 3 groups
Grinder Nuova Simonelli Mythos

Espresso $3.03
Cappuccino $4.04
Latte $4.04

Sister locations Multiple locations

No. 7

Kaffe 1668

401 Greenwich Street, Manhattan, NY 10013 | **Tribeca**

After a leisurely walk in Hudson River Park, there are few better places to relax and refuel than Kaffe 1668 - as long as you can find a seat. At lunchtime especially, this place is crazy-busy. The big, low-lit room is a pleasure to be in, with zany décor dominated by dozens of cute little fluffy sheep. But it isn't the sheep that get people flocking here. The coffee is made to exacting standards even when crowds are huge, and sandwiches, salads and fresh-squeezed juices provide non-caffeinated sustenance of superior quality.

(646) 559-2587
www.kaffe1668.com
Subway A, C, E (Canal St)

MON-FRI. 6:30am - 10:00pm
SAT-SUN. 7:00am - 8:00pm

First opened 2012
Roaster Spectrum Coffees
Machine Synesso MVP Hydra, 3 groups
Grinder Mahlkönig EK 43, Mahlkönig Peak

Espresso $3.25
Cappuccino $4.25
Latte $4.50

Sister locations Lower Manhattan / Midtown

No. 8

La Colombe Coffee Roasters Wall Street

67 Wall Street, Manhattan, NY 10005 | **Financial District**

La Colombe's Wall Street location is a small place that does a lot of takeout business, which increases your chance of finding a free table. And it's a temptation that's easy to give in to; this attractive place, dominated by pale wood, provides a quiet haven on the Financial District's main drag. Latte art is exceptional, as at their other locations, and they serve both cold brew and latte on tap. A combination of the two, called Black and Tan, is a wonderfully zingy and invigorating drink.

(212) 220-0415
www.lacolombe.com
Subway 2, 3 (Wall St)

Sister locations Multiple locations

MON-FRI. 6:00am - 6:30pm
SAT-SUN. 7:00am - 6.30pm

First opened 2016
Roaster La Colombe Coffee Roasters
Machine La Marzocco GB5, 3 groups
Grinder Nuova Simonelli Mythos

Espresso $3.50
Cappuccino $4.50
Latte $4.75

No. 9

Laughing Man Coffee Company

Vesey Street 300 Vesey Street, Manhattan, NY 10282 | **Battery Park City**

Located on the ground floor of an office building, Laughing Man is very much a cafe for those on the move. The service is speedy and attentive; it's the perfect place to grab a quick healthy salad and a craft coffee on your lunch break. They stock a large selection of house blends, varied in flavor from bright and fruity, to rich and chocolaty, and as any true-blue Aussie establishment, they whip up a very memorable flat white. The baby of Australian-born Hollywood heartthrob Hugh Jackman, Laughing Man is focused on ethical sourcing and production, and giving back to the farming families and communities. Which means you can eat those pastries guilt-free!

Sister locations Duane Street

MON-FRI. 6:30am - 5:00pm
SAT-SUN. 9:00am - 5:00pm

First opened 2012
Roaster Laughing Man Coffee Company
Machine Faema E61 Legend, 2 groups
Grinder Nouva Simonelli Mythos, Mazzer Luigi

Espresso	$3.00
Cappuccino	$4.25
Latte	$4.75

(212) 680-1111
www.laughingmancafe.com
Subway A (Chambers St) or J, Z, 4, 5 (Fulton St) or N, R, W (Cortland St)

No. 10

Laughing Man Coffee Company

Duane Street 184 Duane Street, Manhattan, NY 10014 | **Tribeca**

This tiny Tribeca cafe serves up an excellent cup of coffee for a great cause. Inspired by a trip to Ethiopia, Hugh Jackman opened the first Laughing Man in order to provide a market for coffee farmers in developing countries. The cafe is quite crowded during peak hours, but it serves only as a testament to the quality of their roasts, and the wait is always worth it. The best part - one hundred percent of Hugh Jackman's proceeds are donated to the Laughing Man Foundation, supporting social entrepreneurs around the world.

(212) 680-1111
www.laughingmancafe.com
Subway 1, 2, 3 (Chambers St)

Sister locations Battery Park City

MON-SUN. 6:00am - 7:00pm

First opened 2010
Roaster Laughing Man Coffee Company
Machine La Marzocco Strada AV, 2 groups
Grinder Nuova Simonelli Mythos Clima Pro

Espresso	$3.00
Cappuccino	$4.30
Latte	$4.35

Nobletree Coffee

185 Greenwich Street, Manhattan, NY 10006 | **Financial District**

Located in the heart of the Financial District at the 4 World Trade Center building, the shop is designed for orders to-go. Nobletree is unique in that it is a roastery first, with beans being roasted fresh in the cafe, right in front of customers. Coffee offerings appear on a rotating menu of single-origins, along with coffee from Nobletree's farms, of course. Whether you are in the mood for a refreshing cold brew or a skillfully pulled espresso, you can never go wrong with a Nobletree brew. What this location lacks in size it more than makes up for in style and coffee quality.

(718) 643-6080
www.nobletreecoffee.com
Subway N, R, W (Cortlandt St) or 1 (WTC Cortlandt)

MON-FRI. 7:00am - 6:00pm
SAT-SUN. 10:00am - 7:00pm

First opened 2017
Roaster Nobletree Coffee Roasters
Machine Modbar, 2 groups, La Marzocco, 2 groups
Grinder Mahlkönig EK 43, Mahlkönig Peak

Espresso $2.50
Cappuccino $4.50
Latte $3.50

Sister locations Red Hook

No. 12

R&R Coffee

76 Fulton Street, Manhattan, NY 10038 | **Financial District**

Photo: Jael Marschner

Wall Street is on its doorstep, but in spirit and atmosphere R&R is more akin to the Fulton Street Market, also just a step away. Far from being a slick, money-talks kind of Financial District operation, this is a laid-back neighborhood place - more Main Street than Wall Street. Coffee comes from a changing selection of roasters, such as Intelligentsia and Ceremony. It's crafted with care and includes stunning latte art. There's also an extensive list of cold drinks. Bought-in baked goods are rich enough to make love handles at first sight.

(646) 449-8908
randr.coffee
Subway 2, 3 (Fulton St)

MON-FRI. 7:00am - 6:00pm
SAT-SUN. 8:00am - 4:00pm

First opened 2011
Roaster Intelligentsia Coffee, 49th Parallel Coffee Roasters, Forty Weight Coffee Roasters, Ceremony Coffee Roasters
Machine La Marzocco GB5, 3 groups
Grinder Mahlkönig EK 43

Espresso $2.99
Cappuccino $4.36
Latte $4.36

No. 13

Two Hands Tribeca

251 Church Street, Manhattan, NY 10013 | **Tribeca**

Two Hands deserves a loud clap for looks, variety, and vibe. This big Tribeca room looks great and hums with activity from a crowd that seems mostly locals rather than workers. The owners are Australian, and the menu does the whole Oz thing - make it healthy, but make it look and taste great - very well. Grab a table if you're eating. But if you just crave a well-made coffee and some quality time with your smartphone, settle in at the bar in the back of the room.

www.twohandsnyc.com
Subway A, C, E (Canal St)

Sister locations Nolita / Williamsburg (coming soon) / Noho (coming soon)

MON-SUN. 8:00am - 5:00pm

First opened 2016
Roaster Café Integral
Machine La Marzocco Strada, 2 groups
Grinder Mahlkönig K30 Vario

Espresso	$3.50
Cappuccino	$4.50
Latte	$5.00

Voyager Espresso

110 William Street, Manhattan, NY 10038 | **Financial District**

Ignore the address: the easiest way to find Voyager is through the John Street subway exit. However you get here, it's well worth the voyage. This unlikely location houses one of the most distinctively elegant-looking coffee spots in town - the silver-painted chipboard is particularly unique. More importantly, it houses seriously terrific espresso drinks. They roast their own beans, and get fabulous results through expert handling. If you love coffee (and talking about coffee with friendly baristas), Voyager is a genius subterranean heaven.

(212) 227-2744
www.voyagerespresso.com
Subway 2, 3, 4, 5, A, C (Fulton St)

MON-FRI.	7:30am - 4:00pm
SAT-SUN.	Closed

First opened 2015
Roaster Voyager Espresso
Machine Synesso MVP Hydra, 3 groups
Grinder Mahlkönig K30, Mahlkönig EK 43

Espresso	$2.50
Cappuccino	$4.75
Latte	$4.75

No. 15

The Wooly Daily

11 Barclay Street, Manhattan, NY 10007 | **Financial District**

If you weren't smiling before you walked into The Wooly Daily, you certainly will be inside. This place is a hoot to look at, with more decorative features in its box-size space than you'd have thought possible. The food offering is not large, just a few sandwiches and some serious in-house-baked sweetness, but the coffee offering - beans from Coffee Manufactory - is excellent. Like the whole operation, it will make you smile - well, it should make you smile. If you're wondering about the name, look up: the cafe is on the ground floor of the Woolworth Building, formerly the tallest building in the world.

(212) 571-2930
www.thewoolydaily.com
Subway 2, 3 (Park Pl) or N, R, W (City Hall)

MON-THU.	7:00am - 6:00pm
FRI.	7:00am - 5:00pm
SAT-SUN.	Closed

First opened 2015
Roaster Coffee Manufactory
Machine La Marzocco Linea, 2 groups
Grinder Mazzer Luigi Super Jolly, Mazzer Luigi Major E

Espresso	$3.25
Cappuccino	$4.25
Latte	$4.75

No. 16

The East Village and surrounding areas all have a laidback, colourful vibe. Tompkins Square Park in Alphabet City and the range of vibrant off-Broadway theaters in the East Village are worth a visit, while the Lower East Side is packed with trendy shops, vintage stores, contemporary art galleries, rich local history and vibrant nightlife. The neighborhood still retains much of its Jewish heritage in the buildings, restaurants and synagogues that were established by immigrant communities during the 20th century.

East Village & Lower East Side

Abraço

81 East 7th Street, Manhattan, NY 10003 | **East Village**

When Abraço moved to its current location from a closet-sized space just down the street, it became one of the most serious coffee destinations in downtown Manhattan. Not that it wasn't serious before: it has always had a lively local community packed in for expertly crafted drinks from the company's own roaster. The new space is big, airy, and attractive - terrific for anything from solo sipping to coffee conversation in a big group. Coffee tourists from as far afield as Japan and Australia come here to get that very special Abraço taste. Get something sweet with your drip or espresso, and hang out for a while. Did you know Abraço means hug in Portuguese? The name says a lot.

www.abraconyc.com
Subway 4, 6 (Astor Pl)

MON.	Closed
TUE-SAT.	8:00am - 10:00pm
SUN.	9:00am - 6:00pm

First opened 2007
Roaster Abraço
Machine La Marzocco GB5, 2 groups, La Marzocco Linea, 2 groups
Grinder Mazzer Luigi Robur E

Espresso	$2.00
Cappuccino	$4.00
Latte	$4.50

No. 17

Blue Bottle Coffee Clinton Street

71 Clinton Street, Manhattan, NY 10002 | **Lower East Side**

Blue Bottle continues its relentless expansion, and this Lower East Side incarnation shows how adaptable it is to each venue. The place isn't huge, but it's made to seem spacious by huge windows on two sides. Happily, it isn't just a pick-up-and-leave place but a true neighborhood hangout, with friends and young parents parking themselves for some conversation and R&R. Milky drinks are always fabulous at Blue Bottle, and the pour overs highlight the quality of the roasting. A beautiful, new and untraditional find in the Lower East Side.

(510) 653-3394
bluebottlecoffee.com
Subway F (Delancey St) or M, J, Z (Essex St)

MON-FRI.	7:00am - 6:00pm
SAT-SUN.	7:30am - 6:00pm

First opened 2017
Roaster Blue Bottle Coffee
Machine La Marzocco Linea PB, 2 groups
Grinder Baratza

Espresso	$3.50
Cappuccino	$4.50
Latte	$5.00

Sister locations Multiple locations

No. 18

Bluestone Lane Astor Place

51 Astor Place, Manhattan, NY 10003 | **East Village**

Photo: Ben Hider

Forming part of the major rejuvenation of Astor Place, this Bluestone Lane venue with plenty of seating inside is a lovely spot to meet for brunch and enjoy watching the traffic pass by. Designed with the brand in mind, the glass storefront affords beautiful natural light, creating a bright and inviting space. Whether you are grabbing a fresh baked pastry on the go, or settling in to a relaxed avo smash brunch, Bluestone Lane Astor Place hits the spot with their simple yet absolutely delicious menu.

(718) 374-6858
bluestonelane.com
Subway 6 (Astor Pl)

Sister locations Multiple locations

MON-FRI.	6:30am - 7:30pm
SAT-SUN.	8:00am - 6:30pm

First opened 2016
Roaster Bluestone Lane
Machine La Marzocco Linea, 3 groups x2
Grinder Mazzer Luigi Robur E

Espresso	$3.20
Cappuccino	$4.25
Latte	$4.25

No. 19

Café Grumpy Lower East Side

13 Essex Street, Manhattan, NY 10002 | **Lower East Side**

We're not sure how many visits it takes before you get greeted by name in this tiny place, but we do know that most customers seem to have met the minimum. The very un-grumpy welcome is at its warmest here, from the big smile to always-remembered regular orders to advice about which baked goods to order. ('Do you want healthy or sweet?') All this comes with expertly pulled shots, great latte art and fabulous brewed coffees. 'We want to add to the community,' says the staff here. And they certainly do.

(212) 777-7515
cafegrumpy.com
Subway F (East Broadway & Rutgers St)

MON-FRI. 7:00am - 7:00pm
SAT-SUN. 7:30am - 7:00pm

First opened 2011
Roaster Café Grumpy
Machine Synesso MVP Hydra, 2 groups
Grinder Nuova Simonelli Mythos, Ditting 804

Espresso $3.75
Cappuccino $4.50
Latte $5.00

Sister locations Multiple locations

No. 20

Caffe Vita Coffee Roasting Co.

Lower East Side 124 Ludlow Street, Manhattan, NY 10002 | **Lower East Side**

Caffe Vita's Lower East Side operation is a tiny but trendy hole in the wall, with seating for three people. If you're lucky enough to sit, you'll enjoy watching an exemplary operation at work. The baristas make cup after cup for thirsty locals, many of them regulars, while talking, filling growlers and tending lovingly to the gleaming Kees machine. Vita has its origins on the West Coast, and the pedigree shows in the effortless combination of hip, friendly, casual, and ultra-professional.

(212) 260-8482
www.caffevita.com
Subway F, M, J, Z (Delancey St)

MON-FRI. 7:00am - 9:00pm
SAT-SUN. 8:00am - 9:00pm

First opened 2012
Roaster Caffe Vita Coffee Roasting Co.
Machine Kees van der Westen Spirit, 3 groups
Grinder Mazzer Luigi Robur E

Espresso	$3.50
Cappuccino	$4.75
Latte	$5.00

Sister locations Bushwick

City of Saints Coffee Roasters

Astor Cafe 79 East 10th Street, Manhattan, NY 10003 | **East Village**

With its extremely friendly service and thoughtful but effortless design (lots of wood and epiphytes), City of Saints is remarkably welcoming and relaxed for the often sharp-edged, fast-paced East Village neighborhood. Go for a single-origin cold brew - they roast their own beans in Bushwick - and skip the milk to fully taste its light, floral, black-tea-esque complexity. If you're in the mood for something sweet, try the lavender agave latte (available hot or iced), which has a nice rosemary flavor peeking out behind the agave.

(646) 590-1624
www.cityofsaintscoffee.com
Subway 4, 6 (Astor Pl) or N, Q, R, W (8th St - NYU)

MON-FRI.	7:00am - 7:00pm
SAT.	8:00am - 6:00pm
SUN.	9:00am - 5:00pm

First opened 2014
Roaster City of Saints Coffee Roasters
Machine Modbar, 3 groups
Grinder Nuova Simonelli Mythos Clima Pro

Espresso	$3.00
Cappuccino	$4.50
Latte	$5.00

Sister locations Bushwick

No. 22

Coffee Project New York East Village

239 East 5th Street, Manhattan, NY 10003 | **East Village**

Knowledgeable baristas pull meticulously crafted shots at this quiet East Village shop, serving a combo of their own micro-roasted coffee, as well as a selection of guest roasters on their pour over bar. The shop and the staff are well established within the community of this neighborhood, treating everyone who walks in the door like an old friend rather than a customer. With a unique and interesting house specialty menu, including build your own lattes and a variety of other coffee concoctions, Coffee Project New York is well worth the trek from the subway.

(212) 228-7888
coffeeprojectny.com
Subway 6 (Astor Pl) or B, D, F, M (Broadway Lafayette)

MON-FRI.	7:00am - 6:00pm
SAT.	8:30am - 6:00pm
SUN.	8:30am - 5:30pm

First opened 2015
Roaster Coffee Project New York and guests
Machine La Marzocco Linea PB, 2 groups
Grinder Mahlkönig Peak

Espresso	$3.25
Cappuccino	$4.25
Latte	$4.75

No. 23

Everyman Espresso East Village

136 East 13th Street, Manhattan, NY 10003 | **East Village**

Everyman shares its space with the lobby of the Classic Stage Company theater, but to say that it's the best theater-lobby coffee you've ever had would not do this place justice. This is a serious coffee shop in its own right; the fact that Meryl Streep might brush past your table on her way into the theater is merely a pleasant side effect. Everyman baristas are fanatical, expert and approachable, while the Counter Culture espresso is smooth and reliable. Everyman is a must visit.

www.everymanespresso.com
Subway L (3rd Ave) or 4, 5, 6, L, N, Q, R, W (Union Sq)

Sister locations Soho / Park Slope

MON-SUN. 7:00am - 7:00pm

First opened 2007
Roaster Counter Culture Coffee
Machine La Marzocco Linea, 2 groups
Grinder Nuova Simonelli Mythos One Clima Pro

Espresso	$3.75
Cappuccino	$4.75
Latte	$5.25

No. 24

Frisson Espresso East Village

36 3rd Avenue, Manhattan, NY 10003 | **East Village**

Reasons to love Frisson: 1. It's home to some of the most refined latte art in New York, with a Brazilian-dominant medium roast house blend creating a canvas for smooth, caramel-esque espressos. It's equally glorious served straight up or with a dash of silky milk to soften the hit. 2. Floor to ceiling windows open up the petite L-shaped store and provide front row seats to bustling Third Avenue. Snag a countertop stool and indulge your inner voyeur.

(646) 490-6445
frissonespresso.com
Subway L (3rd Ave)

Sister locations Hell's Kitchen

MON-SUN. 8:00am - 7:00pm

First opened 2018
Roaster Dallis Bros. Coffee
Machine Synesso Cyncra, 3 groups
Grinder Compak K10

Espresso	$3.00
Cappuccino	$4.00
Latte	$4.50

No. 25

Gasoline Alley Coffee Noho

325 Lafayette Street, Manhattan, NY 10012 | **Noho**

Gasoline Alley's Lafayette Street location is the perfect place to pop in and refuel during a long day of shopping. The warehouse aesthetic is made chic - fitting in effortlessly with the Noho vibe. Customers flow in and out of this busy shop, whose stripped down seasonal menu prides quality above all else. Those with a sweet tooth ought to pair their beverage with a delicious chocolate chip cookie. During the summer heat, this shop serves a small selection of refreshing organic iced teas.

www.gasolinealleycoffee.com
Subway 6 (Bleecker St) or B, D, F, M (Broadway - Lafayette St)

Sister locations Soho / Flatiron / West Village

MON-FRI. 7:00am - 7:00pm
SAT-SUN. 8:00am - 7:00pm

First opened 2011
Roaster Intelligentsia Coffee
Machine La Marzocco GB5, 3 groups
Grinder Mazzer Luigi Robur E

Espresso $3.00
Cappuccino $4.25
Latte $4.50

No. 26

Hi-Collar

214 East 10th Street, Manhattan, NY 10003 | **East Village**

This wondrous concept shop specializes in variety of both taste and form. At night, this elegantly designed space transforms into a sake bar, but during the day it focuses on coffee with lots of choice. You're handed a beautifully bound menu when you sit at the sleek 13-seat bar, lit by stained glass lamps above. Flip through and you'll find a special house blend and multiple single origin coffees from a variety of roasters. Hi-Collar offers six different manual brewing options, so you can adventure through processes and tastes.

(212) 777-7018
www.hi-collar.com
Subway 4, 6 (Astor Pl) or L (1st Ave)

SUN-THU.	11:00am - 5:00pm | 6:00pm - 12:00am
FRI-SAT.	6:00pm - 1:00am

First opened 2013
Roaster Multiple roasters
Grinder Ditting 804, Bonmac BM450

Irving Farm New York Lower East Side

TOP 40

88 Orchard Street, Manhattan, NY 10002 | **Lower East Side**

It's Saturday morning brunch rush, and every coffee spot is slammed, but you live downtown and need your cold brew and avocado toast fix. Look no further. Maybe it's 6pm, you just left the office and want a quick pick-me-up prior to dinner. Irving Farm on Orchard is your answer. They offer a rotating menu of single origin coffees, all quite unique in flavor, but still rich and robust. Make the most of the distinct flavor profiles by opting for one of their pour overs or cool down with a smooth but potent cold brew. Consistently speedy and never short of space, this is Lower Manhattan authenticity at its best.

(212) 206-0707
irvingfarm.com
Subway F, J, M, Z (Delancey - Essex St) or N, R, W (Cortland St)

MON-SUN. 7:00am - 7:00pm

First opened 1996
Roaster Irving Farm New York
Machine La Marzocco Linea PB, 2 groups
Grinder Nuova Simonelli Mythos One Clima Pro

Espresso	$3.25
Cappuccino	$4.50
Latte	$4.75

Sister locations Multiple locations

No. 28

La Colombe Coffee Roasters Noho

400 Lafayette Street, Manhattan, NY 10003 | **Noho**

La Colombe's big Noho location always seems to be packed, day or evening. The lines get particularly enormous in the spacious, and very beautiful corner room during the lunch rush, but ample staffing levels and good systems keep them moving through at a reasonable pace. Grabbing a table is a different matter, not that customers ordering to go will care about that. What draws them in is really fine coffee, with single-origin espresso, drip and pour over given special prominence. Despite plenty of competition, La Colombe remains a high flyer.

(212) 677-5834
www.lacolombe.com
Subway 4, 6 (Astor Pl) or N, Q, R, W (8th St - NYU)

Sister locations Multiple locations

MON-FRI. 7:30am - 6:30pm
SAT-SUN. 8:30am - 6:30pm

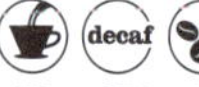

First opened 2011
Roaster La Colombe Coffee Roasters
Machine La Marzocco GB5, 4 groups
Grinder Nuova Simonelli Mythos

Espresso	$3.50
Cappuccino	$4.50
Latte	$4.75

No. 29

The Lazy Llama Coffee Bar

72 East 1st Street, Manhattan, NY 10002 | **East Village**

This offshoot of Hell's Kitchen's The Jolly Goat has a name that fits its leisurely vibe. In the warm months, the tiny shop's front windows swing open and the whole place feels like it's outdoors. Serving Devoción roasted espresso and a lovely drip, the delicious coffee goes hand in hand with its stripped back decor of reclaimed wood and copper tables. A handy, user-friendly drawing on the chalk board above the bar explains the difference between a latte, flat white, macchiato, etc. Order a silky, rich cold brew (sometimes single-origin) and watch the East Village rush by.

(646) 410-1938
Subway F (2nd Ave)

MON-SUN. 7:00am - 6:00pm

First opened 2016
Roaster Devoción,
Machine La Marzocco GB5 EE, 2 groups
Grinder Mazzer Luigi Major

Espresso	$3.25
Cappuccino	$4.25
Latte	$4.50

Sister locations The Jolly Goat

No. 30

Little Canal

26 Canal Street, Manhattan, NY 10002 | **Lower East Side**

At the corner of Essex and Canal, steps away from the F train, sits Little Canal. Large windows on two sides create a sort of fishbowl effect, offering patrons a lovely view of bustling Canal Street. Prepare to be greeted by friendly staff as they pull perfect espresso and craft each cup of coffee with care. At night, the venue transforms into a full-service coffee and wine bar that stays open to serve the bustling Soho streets well into the evening - and even into the early hours sometimes! Compact Little Canal is the sort of cafe that strikes a perfect balance with its ambiance - lively without ever feeling overcrowded.

(917) 472-7479
www.littlecanal.coffee
Subway F (East Broadway Rutgers St) or B, D (Grand St)

MON.	7:00am - 8:00pm
TUE-FRI.	7:00am - 12:00am
SAT.	7.30am - 12:00am
SUN.	7:30am - 8:00pm

First opened 2015
Roaster Madcap Coffee Company
Machine La Marzocco Linea PB, 2 groups
Grinder Mahlkönig Peak, Mahlkönig EK 43

Espresso	$3.00
Cappuccino	$4.00
Latte	$4.50

No. 31

Ludlow Coffee Supply

176 Ludlow Street, Manhattan, NY 10002 | **Lower East Side**

Ludlow Coffee Supply's excellent espresso from D'Amico is so strong that their latte (made with Battenkill Milk) tastes like some of the best cortados you might have had. But the real standout is the bourbon vanilla latte - made with real vanilla and bourbon, and almost no added sugar, which once and for all dispels the notion that a vanilla latte shouldn't be a drink of choice. With great background music and free WiFi, this is a great place to sit with your laptop and get some work done, or relax into their comfortable sofas out the back with a delicious latte and a good book.

(917) 472-7632
www.ludlowcoffeesupply.com
Subway F (Delancey St)

MON-SUN. 7:00am - 9:00pm

First opened 2016
Roaster D'Amico Coffee Roasters
Machine La Marzocco GB5 EE, 2 groups
Grinder Mazzer Luigi Kony E

Espresso $3.25
Cappuccino $3.75
Latte $4.00

Sister locations Williamsburg

Ninth Street Espresso East Village

341 East 10th Street, Manhattan, NY 10009 | **East Village**

Ninth Street Espresso is featured regularly in lists of New York's best espresso, and there's good reason for this reputation: the coffee is awesome. Ninth Street has been doing its own roasting since 2013, and total control from green beans to pulled shots yields beautiful results. There are tables at the front of this small location, but sitting at the bar gives you the chance to talk to the friendly - and exceptionally skilled - baristas.

(646) 861-1440
www.ninthstreetespresso.com
Subway L (1st Ave)

Sister locations Multiple locations

MON-SUN. 7:00am - 7:00pm

First opened 2008
Roaster Ninth Street Roasting
Machine La Marzocco GB5 EE, 2 groups
Grinder Mahlkönig Guatemala

Espresso	$3.50
Cappuccino	$4.50
Latte	$4.50

No. 33

Ost Cafe

511 Grand Street, Manhattan, NY 10002 | **Lower East Side**

You feel at home the instant you walk through the door of Ost. Set in the first floor of an old Lower East Side building, the space preserves the spirit of the early 20th century while the coffee brewing is right up to date - beans from PT's in Topeka, Kansas, and gorgeous latte art. With grand windows providing a view of the street outside, you can spend a very restful interlude with your coffee, a piece of cake, and a good book (or your phone, if you insist). An absolute pleasure, and much needed in this area.

(516) 808-4764
www.ostcafenyc.com
Subway M (Essex St) or F (East Broadway)

MON-FRI. 7:30am - 7:00pm
SAT-SUN. 8:00am - 7:00pm

First opened 2013
Roaster PT's Coffee Roasting Co.
Machine La Marzocco Linea, 2 groups
Grinder Mazzer Luigi Robur E

Espresso	$2.50
Cappuccino	$4.00
Latte	$4.25

No. 34

The Roost

222 Avenue B, Manhattan, NY 10009 | **East Village**

The Roost ticks so many Lower East Side boxes you'd think they had an algorithm for peak hipsterdom. Bare brick, distressed wood, gleaming tiles, craft beers, cool cocktails, Balthazar pastries - it's all here. But if it sounds calculating, it comes across as friendly and sincere. Service is sweet, and rather than pushing customers in the direction of milky espresso-based drinks, they make a big feature of their single-origin coffees brewed or made in the French press. At night The Roost is a bar, and understandably, it gets crowded.

(646) 918-6700
newyork.theroostnyc.com
Subway L (Union Sq)

MON-SUN. 7:00am - 2:00am

First opened 2014
Roaster The Roost Coffee Co.
Machine La Marzocco Linea, 2 groups
Grinder Mahlkönig

Espresso	$3.00
Cappuccino	$4.00
Latte	$4.25

No. 35

Round K

99 Allen Street, Manhattan, NY 10002 | **Lower East Side**

There are so many lovable quirks about Round K, it seems unfair to highlight one above the others. The décor is nonstop fun, even in the restroom, and the little roaster in the window makes an instant talking point. But the sight of owner, Ockhyeon, making scrambled eggs using the steam wand of his gleaming Arduino wins our deepest devotion for off-the-wall eccentricity. It's used in various all-day breakfast dishes, bundled into set menus with a house brew and a small yogurt. The espresso blend is brisk, punchy, and best with milk. And even if you don't have any espresso machine eggs, it's nice to know they're there.

(917) 475-1423
www.roundk.com
Subway F (Delancey St) or B, D (Grand St)

MON-WED.	8:00am - 10:00pm
THU-FRI.	8:00am - 12:00am
SAT.	9:00am - 12:00am
SUN.	9:00am - 10:00pm

First opened 2015
Roaster Round K Coffee Roasters
Machine Victoria Arduino Athena Leva, 2 groups
Grinder Mazzer Luigi M100, Mazzer Luigi Major

Espresso	$3.00
Cappuccino	$3.75
Latte	$4.00

No. 36

Saltwater Coffee

345 East 12th Street, Manhattan, NY 10003 | **East Village**

Saltwater Coffee is a beautifully unassuming Aussie outpost serving coffee from Sydney's Little Marionette Coffee Roasters. With white walls, marble counter tops, and light wood, you're transported to a beachside cafe the moment you walk through the door. If you do manage to snag one of the limited seats, you'll be treated to a hip spot to chill and sip. Their pour overs and turmeric lattes stand out, but don't pass up the chance to sample a skilfully pulled and poured flat white. While the coffee might be far from its Australian home, everything else about this shop is as comfortable and inviting as that famous Aussie charm.

(917) 881-2245
saltwaternyc.com
Subway L (1st Ave)

MON-FRI.	7:00am - 7:00pm
SAT-SUN.	8:00am - 7:00pm

First opened 2017
Roaster The Little Marionette Coffee Roasters
Machine La Marzocco Linea PB, 2 groups
Grinder Anfim SP II

Espresso	$3.25
Cappuccino	$4.00
Latte	$4.36

No. 37

Sonnyboy

65 Rivington Street, Manhattan, NY 10002 | **Lower East Side**

This genial all-day gathering spot in the Lower East Side produces seasonally vibrant menus served alongside specialty coffee and Australian accents. Sonnyboy is anchored by a long, welcoming bar spanning its center, with tables topped with plates of harissa folded eggs, seasonal salads and silky espresso drinks underpinning the whole experience. By night the crowds start spilling onto the front patio, but the coffee doesn't end there. Sonnyboy excels in taking coffee from day to night with their 'but, first coffee' cocktail - smoky and chocolatey with tequila, mezcal and draft cold brew - and a textbook espresso martini, which we're a teeny bit in love with.

(212) 431-5200
www.sonnyboynyc.com
Subway J, F (Delancey St - Essex St)

MON. 8:00am - 4:00pm
TUE-SUN. 8:00am - 12:00am

First opened 2019
Roaster Café Integral
Machine La Marzocco Linea PB, 2 groups
Grinder Compak E8

Espresso $3.00
Cappuccino $4.00
Latte $4.50

Sister locations Banter

No. 38

Supermoon Bakehouse

120 Rivington Street, Manhattan, NY 10002| **Lower East Side**

Industrial and sugary sweet, Supermoon is our favorite cafe for serious eye candy. Walking in feels like entering a patisserie of the future thanks to Aron Tzimas' cheeky design, with a neon 'Bite me, NYC' sign. Counter Culture Coffee is prepared on the sleek Modbar and served in baby pink mugs with latte art to match the beautifully crafted row of pastries displayed on the marble bar. While it may sound like another savvy Instagram trap, these pastries go way beyond visuals. So you can post a photo of your Lychee Berry Jelly Bi-Color Croissant and eat it too!

www.supermoonbakehouse.com
Subway J, Z, F (Delancey St - Essex St)

MON-THU.	8:00am - 10:00pm
FRI.	8:00am - 11:00pm
SAT.	9:00am - 11:00pm
SUN.	9:00am - 10:00pm

First opened 2017
Roaster Parlor Coffee
Machine Modbar, 1 group
Grinder Mahlkönig K30 Air

Espresso	$3.00
Cappuccino	$4.00
Latte	$4.50

Three Seat Espresso

137 Avenue A, Manhattan, NY 10009 | **East Village**

Beyond great coffee served alongside fresh bites, the appeal of this Aussie cafe is the hang culture. Everyone here seems to be a regular, and with coffee this good, we know why. Opened by Aaron Cook, a key player in shaping New York's Australian coffee scene, Three Seat Espresso was built to foster a culture of belonging with local residents, and Aaron's consistent presence in the space as owner-operator has resulted in an exceptional emphasis on quality of product and service. High top seats in the front offer the perfect perch for a quick cup and views of Tompkins Square Park through double frontage glass windows, while the back room, glowing pink, offers a more intimate space for dining on elevated iterations of bagels and loaded toasts, including not one but two versions of avocado toast.

Lemon yellow dine-in and takeaway cups speak of sunshine and summer, creating a warm atmosphere all year round. If you're duly caffeinated, Three Seat also has a generous variety of teas and specialty lattes, including a spicy beet latte which is earthy and rich. You can also add CBD for some extra chill, or switch over to their rotating selection of beer or wine and sit back as the sun sets behind the trees.

No. 40

MON-FRI. 7:00am - 5:00pm
SAT-SUN. 8:00am - 5:00pm

First opened 2016
Roaster East One Coffee Roasters
Machine La Marzocco Linea, 2 groups
Grinder Mahlkönig K30 Vario

Espresso	$3.25
Cappuccino	$4.25
Latte	$4.25

(917) 274-9263
threeseatespresso.com
Subway L (1st Ave) or 4, 6 (Astor Pl)

Soho refers to South of Houston Street and is home to some of New York's best shopping with a variety of stores from trendy boutiques and upscale designers to highstreet favorites and chains. Originally an artist's haven before making way for the shopping district, Soho is a firm favorite for residential loft living. Neighboring Nolita (short for North of Little Italy), extends the shopping district and includes some of the best kept secrets.

Soho & Neighboring

Photo: Tyler Nix

About Coffee

71 Sullivan Street, Manhattan, NY 10012 | **Soho**

This snug little cafe on a quiet Soho side street is a great spot to settle down and read or grab a coffee before hitting the busy streets. Serving coffee from upstate New York's Gimme! Coffee, About provides a quality coffee experience, supplemented by a rotating selection of seasonal drinks such as the Lungo Lemon (a delicious sparkling lemonade with espresso) or the classic Caffe Cardamo (a mocha with a special twist). If you're in this neighborhood, you'd be well advised to check out what About is all about.

(212) 219-1408
aboutcoffee.nyc
Subway 1 (Canal St) or C, E (Spring St)

Sister locations Downtown Brooklyn / Upper West Side

MON-SAT.	7:00am - 7:00pm
SUN.	8:00am - 3:00pm

First opened 2016
Roaster Gimme! Coffee
Machine Nuova Simonelli Aurelia II, 2 groups
Grinder Mahlkönig K30 Twin

Espresso	$3.00
Cappuccino	$4.00
Latte	$5.00

Café Grumpy Nolita

177 Mott Street, Manhattan, NY 10012 | **Nolita**

Situated moments away from Little Italy, this Café Grumpy location is the perfect spot to grab your daily dose of caffeine amidst this bustling area on the edge of Chinatown. A bit smaller than other Grumpy locations, this shop facilitates the sort of grab-and-go environment that comes with its busy location. But have no fear, the quality service is never compromised - neither is the exquisite coffee. Pop in for a quality caffeine hit whilst exploring the attractions of Downtown Manhattan.

(212) 226-6810
cafegrumpy.com
Subway 4, 6 (Spring St)

Sister locations Multiple locations

MON-FRI. 7:00am - 7:30pm
SAT-SUN. 7:30am - 7:30pm

First opened 2016
Roaster Café Grumpy
Machine Synesso MVP Hydra, 2 groups
Grinder Nuova Simonelli Mythos x3, Mahlkönig Guatemala, Mazzer Luigi

Espresso	$3.75
Cappuccino	$4.50
Latte	$5.00

No. 42

Café Integral

TOP 40

149 Elizabeth Street, Manhattan, NY 10012 | **Nolita**

With its clean, minimalist aesthetic, Café Integral exudes calm amidst its crowded Nolita location. The smart design maximizes seating, making the shop a comfortable spot to meet with friends. Owner César Martin Vega is committed to serving beautiful Nicaraguan coffees, a promise that is evident as soon as you taste his pour overs. In addition to the Nicaraguan offerings, the cafe has crafted a unique selection of specialty beverages, including the delicious Matcha Fizz and Horchata Latte. One not to be missed!

(305) 458-3769
www.cafeintegral.com
Subway 6 (Spring St) or B, D (Grand St)

MON-FRI. 7:00am - 5:00pm
SAT-SUN. 8:00am - 5:00pm

First opened 2016
Roaster Café Integral
Machine La Marzocco Linea, 2 groups
Grinder Compak F10

Espresso	$3.00
Cappuccino	$4.00
Latte	$4.50

No. 43

Chalait Hudson Square

299 West Houston Street, Manhattan, NY 10014 | **Hudson Square**

The setting of this Chalait branch couldn't be more corporate - it's part of the Saatchi & Saatchi HQ - but the feeling inside this big room is anything but soulless.
The serving counters sit in the middle of the room, leaving plenty of space to sit and sip in blissful, WiFi-free solitude. Chalait emphasizes its teas and healthy eating options as much as its skilfully brewed coffees. Beans are from Counter Culture and they perform well both in drip and from the La Marzocco Linea PB. While there is loads of coffee and casual dining competition in the area, Chalait outshines them all.

(646) 922-8436
www.chalait.com
Subway 1, 2 (Houston St)

MON-FRI. 7:00am - 6:00pm
SAT-SUN. 9:00am - 4:00pm

First opened 2015
Roaster Counter Culture Coffee
Machine La Marzocco Linea PB, 2 groups
Grinder Nuova Simonelli Mythos Pro

Espresso $3.25
Cappuccino $4.25
Latte $4.75

Sister locations Upper West Side / Chelsea

No. 44

Charley St

41 Kenmare Street, Manhattan, NY 10012 | **Nolita**

Increasingly, Australian cafes are synonymous with fresh, cool and featuring avocado. Well, welcome to Charley St. This all-day cafe is a great example of fine casual dining with young chef Dan Churchill blending his Australian roots and modern approach to food, creating colorful bowls, toasts and healthy treats with a focus on sustainable, local, and ethical ingredients. This served aside damn good coffee - in a city where finding a great meal and an excellently pulled coffee can feel mutually exclusive - makes Charley St a pretty and unique addition to the New York coffee scene.

(646) 220-2538
www.charleyst.com
Subway J, Z (Bowery) or 6 (Spring St)

MON-FRI. 7:30am - 6:00pm
SAT-SUN. 8:00am - 6:00pm

First opened 2018
Roaster Proud Mary Coffee
Machine La Marzocco GB5
Grinder Mahlkönig K30 Air

Espresso	$3.00
Cappuccino	$3.90
Latte	$3.90

No. 45

Everyman Espresso Soho

301 West Broadway, Manhattan, NY 10013 | **Soho**

Everyman enlivens the statutory bare brick walls with colorful tiles reminiscent of a Mondrian painting, and with well-designed lighting they make the room a visual delight. That would be reason enough to come here, but the drinks - proclaimed as 'Damn Fine Coffee' in lettering on windows, grinders and elsewhere - make a visit even more urgent. The gleaming La Marzocco is used to pull fabulous shots, including single-origin specials. People come with kids, friends, devices and headphones. It's a nice mix, producing a friendly neighborhood cafe with real charm.

www.everymanespresso.com
Subway A, C, E (Canal St)

Sister locations East Village / Park Slope

MON-FRI. 7:30am - 6:00pm
SAT-SUN. 8:00am - 6:00pm

First opened 2013
Roaster Counter Culture Coffee
Machine La Marzocco Strada, 3 groups
Grinder Nuova Simonelli Mythos One Clima Pro x3

Espresso	$3.75
Cappuccino	$4.75
Latte	$5.25

No. 46

Gasoline Alley Coffee Soho

154 Grand Street, Manhattan, NY 10013 | **Soho**

At Gasoline Alley's Soho location, the group-heads on the espresso machine outnumber the seats. Three of one, two of the other. However the irresistible baked goods (dive for a donut if you see one) will certainly sweeten your stay. They need all three groups on the La Marzocco because people pile in for cups to go and everything is made well using Intelligentsia beans. Gasoline Alley provides the fuel for local workers and residents with cheerful efficiency, which they guzzle down eagerly.

(212) 933-0113
www.gasolinealleycoffee.com
Subway 4, 6 (Canal St)

Sister locations Noho / Flatiron / West Village

MON-FRI.	7:00am - 7:00pm
SAT-SUN.	8:00am - 7:00pm

First opened 2011
Roaster Intelligentsia Coffee
Machine La Marzocco GB5, 3 groups
Grinder Mazzer Luigi Robur E

Espresso	$3.00
Cappuccino	$4.25
Latte	$4.50

Gimme! Coffee Nolita

228 Mott Street, Manhattan, NY 10012 | **Nolita**

This Nolita outpost of the Ithaca-based roastery is an unassuming gem. It's nothing flashy, just the model of a local cafe where lots of regulars come through, and everyone gets a warm welcome. Most people come in for drinks to go, but those who drink on the premises get the full benefit of exquisite latte art on the well-made latte and cappuccino. Sit on the bench outside if weather permits and watch the world go by.

(212) 226-4011
gimmecoffee.com
Subway F (2nd Ave)

Sister locations Williamsburg

MON-FRI.	7:00am - 6:00pm
SAT-SUN.	8:00am - 6:00pm

First opened 2008
Roaster Gimme! Coffee
Machine La Marzocco Strada, 2 groups
Grinder Mazzer Luigi Robur, Nuova Simonelli Mythos, Bunn

Espresso	$3.25
Cappuccino	$4.75
Latte	$4.75

No. 48

Greecologies

379 Broome Street, Manhattan, NY 10013 | **Soho**

Greecologies sells fancy yogurt and coffee with grass-fed butter (it's a keto thing). They recently reopened with updates to their fit-out and a renewed coffee program. The space has never looked more fresh (or more Greek) with ample nooks to settle into and a stellar garden out back. If you opt for butter coffee there's a choice of four - classic, raw cocoa, cinnamon, or maca, but they also have traditional coffee options if you want milk instead. If you want to watch yogurt made with traditional Greek methods, they have a viewing window at the center of the space. The result is luscious - try it with walnuts and honey, and pair it with a lovingly crafted cappuccino.

(212) 941-0100
www.greecologies.com
Subway J, Z (Bowery)

MON-FRI. 8:00am - 8:00pm
SAT-SUN. 9:00am - 8:00pm

First opened 2014
Roaster Coperaco Roasters
Machine La Marzocco Linea, 2 groups
Grinder Mahlkönig EK 43,
Mazzer Luigi Robur E

Espresso $3.50
Cappuccino $4.50
Latte $4.50

No. 49

Ground Support Cafe

399 West Broadway, Manhattan, NY 10012 | **Soho**

Shoppers and local creatives comprise a constant stream of devotees to this oasis of great coffee in bustling Soho. If you can't get a seat at one of the rustic picnic tables, don't worry, the bench outside is even more pleasant. You can't go wrong with an espresso drink, but the delicate, nuanced pour over here is truly a must.

(212) 219-8722
www.groundsupportcafe.com
Subway C, E (Spring St) or 4, 6 (Spring St)

MON-FRI. 7:00am - 8:00pm
SAT-SUN. 8:00am - 8:00pm

First opened 2009
Roaster Ground Support
Machine La Marzocco Linea, 3 groups
Grinder Mazzer Luigi Robur E

Espresso $3.50
Cappuccino $4.25
Latte $4.25

No. 50

Happy Bones

394 Broome Street, Manhattan, NY 10013 | **Nolita**

This shop used to be a walk-in refrigerator, if you can believe it, and before that, an alleyway. But with some imaginative design, it's become a fashionable cafe instead. Happy Bones is a neighborhood favorite, popular for flat whites and long blacks, drinks made popular since jumping over from Australia and New Zealand.
The well-defined space is both industrial and elegant in feel, the white palette creates an excellent environment for clearing your thoughts. Happy Bones sports only a few tables, but it's a beautiful spot to grab a drink before exploring the neighborhood.

(212) 673-3754
www.happybonesnyc.com
Subway 4, 6 (Spring St)

MON-FRI. 7:30am - 7:00pm
SAT-SUN. 8:00am - 7:00pm

First opened 2013
Roaster Counter Culture Coffee
Machine La Marzocco FB80, 2 groups
Grinder Nuova Simonelli Mythos

Espresso $3.25
Cappuccino $4.50
Latte $5.00

No. 51

Housing Works Bookstore Cafe & Bar

126 Crosby Street, Manhattan, NY 10012 | **Soho**

This Soho bookstore cafe serves up great coffee for a great cause. The Housing Works Organization is a non-profit that works to combat AIDS and homelessness through advocacy, services, and its businesses. As it is run by volunteers, one hundred percent of the proceeds from the bookstore and the cafe go toward Housing Works' mission. The cafe serves well-prepared Intelligentsia beans alongside baked goods and freshly made sandwiches. It's the perfect spot to curl up with a great read or meet with friends for lunch, all for an amazing cause.

(212) 334-3324
www.housingworks.org/locations/bookstore-cafe

Subway B, D, F, M (Broadway - Lafayette St) or 4, 6 (Bleecker St)

MON-FRI. 10:00am - 9:00pm
SAT-SUN. 10:00am - 6:00pm

First opened 1996
Roaster Intelligentsia Coffee
Machine La Marzocco Linea MP, 2 groups
Grinder Mazzer Luigi Major

Espresso $2.50
Cappuccino $4.00
Latte $4.25

No. 52

Joe & The Juice Soho

161 Prince Street, Manhattan, NY 10036 | **Soho**

With its dim lighting and loud dance music, this spacious New York outpost of the popular Danish coffee-and-juice bar feels more night club than cafe at times. However, that doesn't affect Joe & The Juice's regulars from stopping by to do some work. Alongside your caffeine kick, make sure to try one of their many delicious smoothies for a burst of healthy flavor.

www.joejuice.com
Subway C, E (Spring St) or R, W (Prince St)

Sister locations Multiple locations

MON-FRI. 7:00am - 8:00pm
SAT-SUN. 8:00am - 8:00pm

First opened 2016
Roaster Joe & The Juice
Machine La Marzocco Linea AV, 2 groups
Grinder Nuova Simonelli Mythos One

Espresso $2.70
Cappuccino $4.30
Latte $4.30

No. 53

Maman

239 Centre Street, Manhattan, NY 10013 | **Soho**

NEW

Maman is a cafe and a bakery which endeavors to bring to life childhood favorites from the south of France and North America. Hearty, farm-fresh salads are served in wooden bowls while sandwiches and quiches lay on display to tempt any patron popping in for a coffee. This Soho location is attached to the Maman marché, with white brick walls and unfinished wood tables that are reminiscent of a cottage in the French countryside. Be sure to order one of their famous nutty chocolate chip cookies, named one of Oprah's 'favorite things' for 2017. Who can argue with Oprah?

(212) 226-0700
www.mamannyc.com
Subway N, Q, R, W (Canal St) or 6 (Spring St)

MON-FRI. 7:00am - 6:00pm
SAT-SUN. 8:00am - 8:00pm

First opened 2014
Roaster Partners Coffee
Machine La Marzocco Linea, 2 groups
Grinder Mazzer Luigi

Espresso $3.00
Cappuccino $4.00
Latte $4.50

Sister locations Mutliple locations

No. 54

McNally Jackson Independent Booksellers and Café 52 Prince Street, Manhattan, NY 10012 | **Soho**

Literary lovers will fall head over heels for this charming cafe on the ground floor of McNally Jackson, one of the city's most popular independent bookstores. This cozy space effortlessly blends coffee and culture. Parlor coffee is proudly served, along with a selection of fair trade teas and light fare. It's the perfect spot to start that new book you've been dying to read, and an inspiring location for writers and other creatives to do some work.

(212) 274-1160
www.mcnallyjackson.com/cafe
Subway 4, 6 (Spring St) or N, Q, R, W (Prince St) or B, D, F, M (Broadway - Lafayette St)

MON-SUN. 9:00am - 9:00pm

First opened 2004
Roaster Olas Coffee Co.
Machine La Marzocco Linea FB70, 2 groups
Grinder Mahlkönig EK 43

Espresso	$3.50
Cappuccino	$4.50
Latte	$4.75

No. 55

Now or Never

30 Grand Street, Manhattan, NY 10013 | **Soho**

Now or Never feels like your cool friend's apartment rather than a coffee shop. Having originally operated as a pop-up, the recent relocation to a permanent space on Grand Street has allowed Now or Never to realize their full potential and seriously up their coffee game. The minimal interior design of the space comes alive with the vibrant chatter of staff and patrons, rotating artwork, cult collectibles from Supreme and Tarantino and soothing tunes from the turntable. They're even encouraging local audiophiles to bring along their own vinyl for a spin! Put on your favorite LP and sink into the brown leather sofa if you're staying for a while, otherwise grab a bench by the window to partake in some lunch-break people-watching.

Thanks to a particularly close collaboration with Brooklyn-based Spectrum Coffees, exceptional beans lay the foundation for bright and citrusy coffee. You can't go wrong with a cold brew, or if you want something a little sweeter, they'll make you an affogato served stylishly on a wooden tray, so it doesn't feel like you're eating ice cream for breakfast. They also serve some pretty intriguing baked goods. The matcha and chocolate pastry is an instant hit, and this is our first time seeing a kimchi cookie. Try it now or never!

No. 56

MON-FRI. 7:00am - 6:00pm
SAT-SUN. 8:30am - 4:30pm

First opened 2019
Roaster Spectrum Coffees
Machine La Marzocco Strada, 2 groups
Grinder Mahlkönig EK 43,
Mahlkönig K30 Twin

Espresso	$3.00
Cappuccino	$4.25
Latte	$4.50

(347) 556-8312
now-or-never-coffee-shop.business.site
Subway 1, 2 (Canal St)

Ruby's Soho

219 Mulberry Street, Manhattan, NY 10012 | **Soho**

If Ruby's Mulberry Street restaurant ever has a quiet day, it's never happened when we've been passing by - or trying to get a seat. There's always a bunch of people waiting outside for a taste of Ruby's Aussie-inspired breakfast, brunch, burgers, pasta or salads. Their coffee is carefully brewed from La Colombe beans in filter as well as espresso, though not many people go there for coffee alone (the food is just too good). If it's a nice day, however, and there are a few seats outside, it's a perfect place to sit and sip.

(212) 925-5755
www.rubyscafe.com
Subway N, Q, R, W (Prince St) or 6 (Spring St)

MON-SUN. 9:00am - 10:30pm

First opened 2003
Roaster La Colombe Coffee Roasters
Machine La Marzocco GB5, 2 groups
Grinder Mazzer Luigi Kony E

Espresso	$3.50
Cappuccino	$4.00
Latte	$4.00

Sister locations Murray Hill

No. 57

Saturdays NYC

31 Crosby Street, Manhattan, NY 10013 | **Soho**

Many stores in Manhattan now happen to serve nice coffee, but Saturdays NYC feels like a genuine coffee shop which happens to also be a surf apparel store. This is mostly thanks to a gobsmackingly beautiful, spacious reclaimed-wood backyard, full of tulips, and the fact that it's staffed by folks who truly seem about to go for a surf. La Colombe makes a special blend for their drip; delicious and complex. And on a hot summers day when you might prefer to go for a surf, order a hot black coffee and lounge in the backyard, one of the most pleasant outdoor areas in Manhattan.

(212) 966-7875
www.saturdaysnyc.com
Subway 4, 6 (Canal St)

MON-FRI. 8:00am - 7:00pm
SAT-SUN. 10:00am - 7:00pm

First opened 2009
Roaster La Colombe Coffee Roasters
Machine La Marzocco Linea, 3 groups
Grinder Mazzer Luigi

Espresso $3.00
Cappuccino $4.00
Latte $4.50

Sister locations West Village

Seven Grams Caffé Hudson Square

175 Varick Street, Manhattan, NY 10014 | **Hudson Square**

This breezy, open space nestled in the more high-rise area of Soho offers a casual yet upbeat spot to grab a coffee and a pastry (baked in-house) to-go or to sit and enjoy the spacious and impressively laid-out shop. Growlers and full loaves of house made pound cake mean you can enjoy your coffee and pastries at home as well as in the shop. This is Seven Gram's second location, expanding from their original Chelsea location in late 2017.

(917) 261-7527
www.sevengramscaffe.com
Subway 1 (Houston St)

Sister locations Chelsea / Flatiron

MON-FRI.	7:00am - 7:00pm
SAT.	8:00am - 8:30pm
SUN.	Closed.

First opened 2017
Roaster Seven Grams Caffé
Machine La Marzocco GB5, 3 groups
Grinder Nuova Simonelli Mythos One

Espresso	$3.00
Cappuccino	$4.75
Latte	$4.75

No. 59

Two Hands Nolita

164 Mott Street, Manhattan, NY 10013 | **Nolita**

The laidback attitude at this Aussie-run shop is more than welcome in this busy neighborhood. They've got a full menu of food with favorites like avocado toast and acai bowls, and though the flat white reigns here, all their coffee drinks are good and strong, made with delicious Café Integral coffee. The space is bright and airy with its pristinely white interior and accents of greenery. This is a neighborhood favorite that gets packed on both weekends and weekdays, so hang with other coffee lovers and ride the wave over to this buzzing spot.

www.twohandsnyc.com
Subway B, D (Grand St) or 6 (Spring St)

Sister locations Tribeca / Williamsburg (coming soon) / Noho (coming soon)

MON-SUN. 8:00am - 5:00pm

First opened 2014
Roaster Café Integral
Machine La Marzocco Strada, 2 groups
Grinder Mahlkönig K30 Vario

Espresso	$3.50
Cappuccino	$4.50
Latte	$5.00

No. 60

Photo: Ruby's

Known as 'The Village' to locals, Greenwich village houses some of the most expensive homes in Manhattan. A landmark for bohemian culture, the desirable location is very sought after. Washington Square park is at the center of the neighborhood and provides much needed green space amongst the packed residential quarters. Nestled in the unique streets of the West Village lie many trendy food and coffee spots which offer a local vibe.

West Village & Neighboring

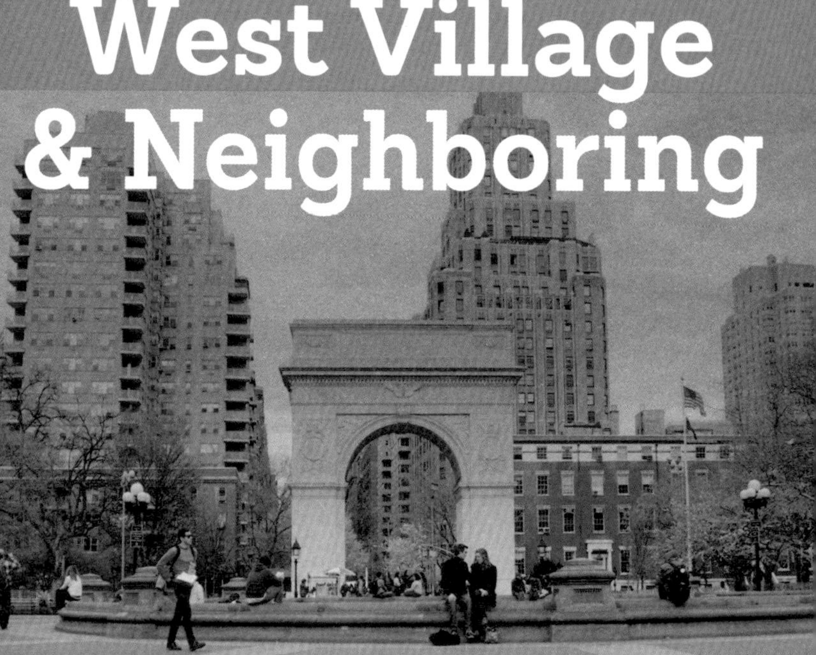

Banter

169 Sullivan Street, Manhattan, NY 10012 | **West Village**

Founded by former Two Hands baristas and Australian natives, Nick Duckworth and Josh Evans, Banter brings together a delicious restaurant menu with a casual sit-down vibe, creating a perfect balance between formal dining and cafe casual. Banter features a health-conscious menu with items popular in both Australia and the US. The light wood interior and airy aesthetic, along with the beautiful prints lining the walls, gives the whole room a friendly, inviting feel, and the beautifully prepared dishes are not to be missed. Added bonus? Their lovely patio offering airy outdoor seating during the warmer months.

www.banternyc.com
Subway C, E (Spring St)

SUN-MON. 8:00am - 4:00pm
TUE-SAT. 8:00am - 11:00pm

First opened 2017
Roaster Café Integral
Machine La Marzocco Strada EE, 2 groups
Grinder Compak F10

Espresso $3.00
Cappuccino $4.00
Latte $4.50

Sister locations Sonnyboy

No. 61

Bluestone Lane Collective Café

55 Greenwich Avenue, Manhattan, NY 10014 | **Greenwich Village**

Photo: Ben Hider

Bluestone Lane does not do unattractive: all its locations are a treat for the eye. But the Collective Café is particularly pretty, especially on a sunny day. The white picket fence might make you think you're in Melbourne or Sydney. The menu will do the same trick, with its Antipodean views of clean and healthy living (including a totally delectable brunch menu). Coffee at Bluestone is never anything less than outstanding: it's just a question of whether you're in the mood for a well-pulled espresso shot or a famous flat white.

(718) 374-6858
bluestonelane.com
Subway 1, 2 (Christopher St - Sheridan Sq) or 1, 2, 3 (14th St)

MON-WED. 8:30am - 6:30pm
THU-SUN. 8:00am - 7:30pm

First opened 2014
Roaster Bluestone Lane
Machine La Marzocco Linea PB, 3 groups
Grinder Mazzer Luigi Robur E

Espresso $3.20
Cappuccino $4.25
Latte $4.25

Sister locations Multiple locations

No. 62

Bluestone Lane West Village

30 Carmine Street, Manhattan, NY 10014 | **West Village**

Photo: Ben Hider

The table service at this West Village branch of Bluestone couldn't be sweeter. And the cafe itself is gleaming with white walls, pale wood flooring and large windows letting in lots of light. The menu features delicious Aussie brunch items, including eggs, avocados and sourdough, with several gluten-free options available. For something different in your cup, try the 'Magic': a double ristretto in a 4.5-ounce cup with steamed and micro-foamed milk.

(718) 374-6858
bluestonelane.com
Subway A, C, E, B, D, F, M (West 4th St)

Sister locations Multiple locations

MON-THU. 8:00am - 6:00pm
FRI-SUN. 8:00am - 7:00pm

First opened 2016
Roaster Bluestone Lane
Machine La Marzocco Linea PB, 3 groups
Grinder Mazzer Luigi Robur E

Espresso $3.20
Cappuccino $4.25
Latte $4.25

No. 63

Jack's Stir Brew Coffee

138 West 10th Street, Manhattan, NY 10014 | **West Village**

Established in 2003, Jack's is an old school favorite amongst the NYC coffee scene. Photographs cover the walls of their 10th Street cafe, giving it a homey atmosphere. It is quiet and serene, the perfect spot to do work or just relax with a great cup of coffee. Community is emphasized at Jack's - baristas know a regular's order as soon as they step up to the counter. Pair your coffee with one of their delicious vegan baked goods, or take a bar of chocolate to-go.

(212) 929-0821
www.jacksstirbrew.com
Subway 1, 2 (Christopher St - Sheridan Sq)

Sister locations Multiple locations

MON-SUN. 6:00am - 6:00pm

First opened 2003
Roaster Jack's Stir Brew Roast
Machine La Marzocco GB5, 2 groups
Grinder Mazzer Luigi

Espresso	$3.25
Cappuccino	$4.50
Latte	$4.50

No. 64

Kava Cafe

803 Washington Street, Manhattan, NY 10014 | **West Village**

This polished coffee bar pulls excellent shots on their sleek La Marzocco Strada, and the filter coffee is notable. Its classical Italian-inspired interior and coffee to match make this Washington Street cafe truly authentic. If you are after something other than coffee then give the beer a try.

(212) 255-7495
www.kavanyc.com
Subway L (8th Ave) or A, C, E (14th St)

MON-FRI. 7:00am - 7:00pm
SAT-SUN. 8:00am - 6:00pm

First opened 2011
Roaster Ceremony Coffee Roasters
Machine La Marzocco Strada, 3 groups
Grinder Mazzer Luigi x2

Espresso	$3.75
Cappuccino	$4.75
Latte	$5.25

No. 65

Kobrick Coffee Co.

24 9th Avenue, Manhattan, NY 10014 | **Meatpacking District**

After roasting beans for nearly a century, Kobrick decided to open a cafe in the trendy Meatpacking District in 2015. Yet it feels as if it might have been there forever, with its tasteful and timeless dark wood décor (look up at the ceiling) and deeply comfortable gentleman's-club-type seating in the small back room. Kobrick makes incredibly good coffee, whether espresso or drip, and the place is open late, with coffee joined by cocktails as the drinks of choice. Kobrick is a little piece of Old Manhattan on Ninth Avenue - more 1920 than 20-whatever.

(212) 255-5588
www.kobrickcoffee.com
Subway A, C, E (14th St)

MON-FRI.	7:00am - 4:00am
SAT-SUN.	8:00am - 4:00am

First opened 2015
Roaster Kobrick Coffee Co.
Machine La Marzocco GB5, 3 groups
Grinder Mahlkönig K30, Mahlkönig Guatemala

Espresso	$3.50
Cappuccino	$4.50
Latte	$5.00

No. 66

Merriweather Coffee + Kitchen

428 Hudson Street, Manhattan, NY 10014 | **West Village**

Inspired by the trendy beach cafes of Australia, Merriweather Coffee + Kitchen is a standout spot in the picturesque West Village. Large windows paired with the light wood and mint green aesthetic generate a vibrant, welcoming space. Counter Culture beans are expertly brewed, and the food menu is as delicious as it is unique, with lots of healthy options across the board, including their popular Merriweather Morning Sandwiches and turmeric ginger oatmeal. There is also a wonderful outdoor bench to perch on if the weather is good. Whether meeting friends for lunch or just in need of a delicious drink to-go, Merriweather is your perfect ray of sunshine.

(646) 678-5678
www.merriweathernyc.com
Subway 1, 2 (Houston St)

MON-FRI. 7:00am - 6:00pm
SAT-SUN. 8:00am - 6:00pm

First opened 2016
Roaster Counter Culture Coffee and guests
Machine La Marzocco Linea PB ABR, 2 groups
Grinder Mahlkönig Peak, Mahlkönig EK 43

Espresso	$3.50
Cappuccino	$4.50
Latte	$4.75

No. 67

Orens Coffee NYU

29 Waverly Place, Manhattan, NY 10003 | **Greenwich Village**

This branch of legendary Orens Coffee could hardly have a better location, with thousands of people at NYU's main campus right on the doorstep. But it's not only caffeine-craving students and professors who benefit here. This is the heart of the Village, and Washington Square Park is one minute away. Grab your brew and go out to watch the passing parade, or grab a seat in the small but attractive cafe. Drip coffee is always good at Orens, and the least expensive drink in the place if you buy the small (but still generous) serving.

(212) 348-5400
www.orenscoffee.com
Subway N, Q, R, W (8th St - NYU)

Sister locations Multiple locations

MON-FRI. 7:00am - 7:00pm
SAT-SUN. Closed

First opened 1993
Roaster Orens Coffee
Machine Slayer Steam, 2 groups
Grinder Mahlkönig Guatemala, Nuova Simonelli Mythos One x2

Espresso	$3.00
Cappuccino	$4.00
Latte	$4.00

No. 68

Partners Coffee West Village

44 Charles Street, Manhattan, NY 10014 | **West Village**

Partners' (formerly Toby's Estate) West Village location began life as an artist's studio almost a century ago, as the huge windows on each side of the V-shaped room suggest. Combined with high ceilings, this creates an airy and spacious feel - a great setting for digging in to their excellent baked stuff from highest quality suppliers, including Ovenly, or relaxing over a breakfast of eggs or granola. The pour-over coffees are outstanding, and showcase the roasting skill at Partners' Brooklyn base. If you crave caffeine enlightenment, go to one of their classes in the training lab downstairs.

(646) 590-1924
www.partnerscoffee.com
Subway 1 (Christopher St - Sheridan Sq) or A, C, E (West 4th St)

MON-SUN. 6:30am - 6:00pm

First opened 2014
Roaster Partners Coffee
Machine La Marzocco Strada EE, 3 groups
Grinder Nuova Simonelli Mythos One

Espresso	$3.25
Cappuccino	$4.00
Latte	$4.75

Sister locations Williamsburg / Long Island City / Bushwick / Vanderbilt Market

No. 69

Porto Rico Importing Co.

201 Bleecker Street, Manhattan, NY 10012 | **Greenwich Village**

Porto Rico is truly a coffee emporium, offering a comprehensive selection of direct-trade beans imported from around the world. Established in 1907, this family-owned coffee store has been passed down through the generations, gathering a loyal following throughout the years. Though not a cafe, head to the coffee bar in the back, where a friendly barista will gladly pour a brew for you. No matter your taste, Porto Rico offers a blend for everyone, as well as selling quality machinery to get the most out of their flavor-filled beans.

(212) 477-5421
www.portorico.com
Subway 1, 2 (Houston St) or A, C, E (Spring St)

MON-FRI.	8:00am - 9:00pm
SAT.	9:00am - 9:00pm
SUN.	12:00pm - 7:00pm

First opened 1907
Roaster Porto Rico Importing Co.
Machine Astoria Perla AEP, 2 groups
Grinder Astoria Robur E

Espresso	$1.75
Cappuccino	$3.85
Latte	$3.85

Sister locations East Village / Lower East Side / Williamsburg

No. 70

Prodigy Coffee

33 Carmine Street, Manhattan, NY 10014 | **West Village**

Prodigy use their own beans that they roast in conjunction with Gotham Coffee Roasters to create their own signature drinks as well as outstanding traditional brews. When it's hot, try the Frostbite (cold brew over shaved ice) or the Snakebite (melted dark chocolate with a shot of espresso), when the weather cools down. With these potions, and their family of seasonal single origins and blends, it's easy to have fun experimenting with your taste of coffee here. The six table shop is handsome, with gilded frames and chandeliers composing the space with a polished flare.

(212) 414-4142
www.prodigycoffee.com
Subway A, C, E, B, D, F, M (West 4th St)

MON-FRI. 7:00am - 7:00pm
SAT-SUN. 8:00am - 7:00pm

First opened 2012
Roaster Prodigy Coffee
Machine La Marzocco Linea EE
Grinder Mazzer Luigi Robur E, Baratza, Bunn

Espresso	$3.54
Cappuccino	$4.36
Latte	$4.63

No. 71

Rebel Coffee

19 8th Avenue, Manhattan, NY 10014 | **West Village**

If you're looking for a place with great coffee and a quiet relaxing atmosphere, Rebel Coffee is the place for you. Situated in a quiet corner of the West Village, it is the perfect spot to get work done while sipping on a latte. Stumptown beans are brewed perfectly on the La Marzocco, pulling espresso that is rich, strong, and full of flavor. Also available are delicious artisan donuts by Underwest Donuts, a New York City delicacy. Homey yet upscale, Rebel Coffee is a great place to unwind.

(917) 261-4299
rebelcoffeenyc.com
Subway A, C, E, L (14th St)

MON-SUN. 7:00am - 7:00pm

First opened 2016
Roaster Stumptown Coffee Roasters
Machine La Marzocco Strada EE, 2 groups
Grinder Mazzer Luigi Kony E

Espresso	$3.50
Cappuccino	$4.25
Latte	$4.50

No. 72

TOP 40

Stumptown Coffee Roasters
Greenwich Village 30 West 8th Street, Manhattan, NY 10011 | **Greenwich Village**

Stumptown found a new home here in 2013, bringing its signature Portland style and meticulously prepared coffees downtown. This former village bookshop now houses Stumptown's library of perfectly prepared coffees. The delicious nitro cold brew is served on tap, with a strong dark and creamy taste reminiscent of a nice Guinness. There's an adjoining brew bar where you can get any coffee made any way you like, and they play kind hosts with regular tastings here too.

(347) 414-7802
www.stumptowncoffee.com
Subway A, C, E, B, D, F, M (West 4th St - Washington Sq)

Sister locations Ace Hotel / Cobble Hill

MON-SUN. 7:00am - 8:00pm

First opened 2013
Roaster Stumptown Coffee Roasters
Machine La Marzocco Strada
Grinder Mazzer Luigi Robur E, Ditting

Espresso $3.25
Cappuccino $4.00
Latte $4.50

No. 73

Third Rail Coffee

240 Sullivan Street, Manhattan, NY 10012 | **Greenwich Village**

Despite being tiny, Third Rail is a comfortable place to sip your coffee, thanks to the genuine, relaxed warmth of the baristas. They always serve ethics-focused, consistently great Counter Culture Coffee beans, complete with exquisite latte art on milky brews, but also rotate a second roaster for pour overs. The lattes are excellent, but if you have time, stay for a pour over.

www.thirdrailcoffee.com
Subway A, C, E, B, D, F, M (West 4th St)

Sister locations East Village

MON-FRI. 7:00am - 8:00pm
SAT-SUN. 8:00am - 8:00pm

First opened 2009
Roaster Counter Culture Coffee and guests
Machine La Marzocco GB5, 2 groups
Grinder Mazzer Luigi Robur E

Espresso $3.75
Cappuccino $4.75
Latte $4.75 / $5.25

Photo: Charley St

Running along the Hudson River, Chelsea is home to the popular green oasis of the High Line, the historic Chelsea Piers, bustling Chelsea Market and busy Hudson Yards. With these fantastic areas offering residents a variety of local charms it's easy to see why Chelsea is one of Manhattan's hotspots. Featuring some of the best dining, nightlife and art galleries in Manhattan, Chelsea is a definite neighborhood to visit.

Chelsea

Photo: Hole in the Wall

Blue Bottle Coffee Chelsea

450 West 15th Street, Manhattan, NY 10014 | **Chelsea**

Photo: Alicia Cho

This pocket-size branch of the San Francisco-based chain is perfectly situated for visits to Chelsea Market or the High Line. The space, originally a loading dock, is cleverly used: the cafe is at street level, while the rear mezzanine accommodates Saturday classes (free of charge) in cupping and home brewing. Blue Bottle roasts at its Williamsburg site, and the beans include both blends and single origins. Whether pulled through the two-group Kees van der Westen or lovingly hand-poured, the coffee is treated like royalty. Blue Bottle is blue chip all the way, right down to its delectable in-house baking.

(510) 653-3394
bluebottlecoffee.com
Subway A, C, E (14th St) or A, C, E (14th St - 8th Ave)

MON-FRI. 7:00am - 6:30pm
SAT-SUN. 8:00am - 6:30pm

First opened 2012
Roaster Blue Bottle Coffee
Machine Kees van der Westen Spirit, 2 groups
Grinder Baratza Forte

Espresso	$3.50
Cappuccino	$4.50
Latte	$5.00

Sister locations Multiple locations

No. 75

The Commons Chelsea

128 7th Avenue, Manhattan, NY 10014 | **Chelsea**

The terrific beans from La Colombe get excellent care in this small, very calm Chelsea local. It places strong emphasis on food, served from breakfast onward through dinner, when you can relax with beer or wine as well as coffee. The owners were the first people selling on the High Line, so they're West Side veterans. Tables outside are a great place to perch in fine weather; and latte art can reach some pretty impressive heights. A remarkable venue.

(212) 929-9333
www.thecommonschelsea.com
Subway A, C, E (14th St) or 1 (18th St)

MON-FRI. 7:00am - 6:00pm
SAT-SUN. 8:00am - 6:00pm

First opened 2011
Roaster La Colombe Coffee Roasters
Machine La Marzocco Linea, 2 groups
Grinder Mazzer Luigi Super Jolly

Espresso $3.25
Cappuccino $5.00
Latte $5.00

Sister locations Motel Morris

No. 76

East One Coffee Roasters Chelsea

170 West 23rd Street, Manhattan, NY 10011 | **Chelsea**

East One's new 1,700-square-foot location with Scandinavian-inspired design tropes of simplicity and functionality allows all focus and complexity to exist within cups and upon plates. Chef Will Ono has taken cafe fare and turned it on its head with a globally influenced menu that runs from morning to night, skillfully balancing generosity and refinement. Expectedly, drinks mirror the elevated food program with coffee director Selina Ullrich and production roaster Emily Wendorff sourcing a global package of single-origin beans and highlighting their intricacy in drip, espresso, cold brew, and pour overs. While the attention to craft is technocratic, the service is benevolent, and the Scandanavian chairs unexpectedly comfortable.

(646) 649-3624
eastonecoffee.com
Subway 1 (23rd St)

MON-FRI. 7:00am - 7:00pm
SAT-SUN. 8:00am - 7:00pm

First opened 2019
Roaster East One Coffee Roasters
Machine Slayer Steam LP, 3 groups, Slayer Steam LP, 2 groups
Grinder Mahlkönig Peak x2, Mahlkönig EKK 43, Mahlkönig K30 Twin

Espresso	$3.25
Cappuccino	$4.25
Latte	$4.50

Sister locations Court Street / Baxter Street

No. 77

Intelligentsia Coffee

180 10th Avenue, Manhattan, NY 10011 | **Chelsea**

This Chicago behemoth has made a home inside the elegant lobby of the High Line Hotel. 'Twas the night before Christmas' was written in an apple orchard that once grew upon these historic grounds, and now you too can wax poetic here with an exceptional coffee in hand. The menu changes often with seasonal offerings and they feature a slow bar in lieu of filter coffee where single origins are brewed with care. We suggest drinking al fresco, as the hotel offers beautiful outdoor spaces where coffee patrons can relax in style.

(212) 933-9736
www.intelligentsiacoffee.com
Subway C, E (23rd St)

Sister locations TWA Hotel

SUN-THU. 7:00am - 6:00pm
FRI-SAT. 7:00am - 7:00pm

First opened 2013
Roaster Intelligentsia Coffee
Machine La Marzocco Strada EP, 3 groups
Grinder Mazzer Luigi Robur E

Espresso $3.50
Cappuccino $4.75
Latte $5.75

No. 78

Joe Coffee Company Pro Shop + HQ

131 West 21st Street, Manhattan, NY 10011 | **Chelsea**

There isn't much seating at Joe's Pro shop, but it's probably not needed as most people seem to come in for something to drink on the go. In spite of its size, it's worth coming in to drink on the premises. This is where Joe does his roasting, an operation you can watch behind the glass panels. And while you're watching, you can talk to your heart's content with baristas who are as eager and as knowledgeable as any in the city. While you're there, stock up on beans.

(212) 924-7400
joecoffeecompany.com
Subway F, M (23rd St)

Sister locations Multiple locations

MON-FRI.	7:30am - 5:30pm
SAT-SUN.	9:00am - 4:00pm

First opened 2012
Roaster Joe Coffee Company
Machine La Marzocco Strada, 2 groups
Grinder Mahlkönig EK 43
Mahlkönig Peak x2

Espresso	$4.00
Cappuccino	$4.00
Latte	$4.00

La Colombe Coffee Roasters 27th St. Terminal Warehouse

601 West 27th Street, Manhattan, NY 10001 | **Chelsea**

La Colombe's spacious Chelsea outpost provides a coffee oasis in an area that doesn't have a great deal of choice. That alone would make it a hit, even without the signature Colombe highlights: a large choice of drinks both hot and cold, efficient service, and simple yet tempting baked goodies. This inspired, minimalist, well designed interior is a great place to stop off at when you're going for a walk along the High Line, just a few minutes away, and definitely worth a trip if you're in the area.

(646) 885-0677
www.lacolombe.com
Subway 7 (34th St - Hudson Yards) or 1 (28th St)

Sister locations Multiple locations

MON-FRI. 7:00am - 7:00pm
SAT-SUN. 8:00am - 7:00pm

First opened 2016
Roaster La Colombe Coffee Roasters
Machine La Marzocco GB5, 3 groups
Grinder Nuova Simonelli Mythos One

Espresso $3.50
Cappuccino $4.50
Latte $4.75

No. 80

Seven Grams Caffé Chelsea

275 7th Avenue, Manhattan, NY 10001 | **Chelsea**

Seven Grams punches way above its weight through an enviable combination of great looks, eager service, and delicious baked goods all made in-house. It would be worth coming here even if the place didn't sell such good coffee - but the coffee is great, small doses of ground Fairtrade beans crowned with latte art that's inventive and highly skilled. Chelsea may have lots of other coffee spots to visit, but you should consider tipping the scales in favor of a visit to this one.

(212) 727-1777
www.sevengramscaffe.com
Subway 1, 2, F, M, A, C, E (23rd St) or N, Q, R, 1 (Penn Stn)

MON-FRI. 7:00am - 7:00pm
SAT-SUN. 8:00am - 7:00pm

First opened 2014
Roaster Seven Grams Caffé
Machine La Marzocco GB5, 3 groups
Grinder Nuova Simonelli Clima Pro, Mazzer Luigi

Espresso $3.00
Cappuccino $4.75
Latte $4.75

Sister locations Hudson Square / Flatiron

No. 81

Starbucks Reserve Roastery

61 9th Avenue, Manhattan, NY 10011 | **Chelsea**

If there were such a thing as a coffee theme park (dare to dream), it would take note from Starbucks Reserve. With locations in Milan, Tokyo and Shanghai, New York, the city where the majority of the populous is 90% water 10% caffeine, seemed like a logical progression. The New York Roastery is an immersive performance in the journey of coffee; a workshop and a stage. Watch as bags of green coffee ascend from the cellar via hooks (a nod to the roastery's location in the Meatpacking District), or descend to the cellar yourself to discover a lush terrarium inspired by Starbucks' own coffee farm in Costa Rica, Hacienda Alsacia.

Explore the three levels of this generous, industrial yet elegant space to watch Master Roasters, mixologists and baristas craft and coax flavorful, often unexpected beverages from Starbucks' rarest single-origin coffees. It's a must-visit for any coffee connoisseur, best enjoyed with a friend to share in an Origin or cold brew flight, allowing you to really taste the different notes of the beans roasted on-site. And with coffee-inspired cocktails at Arriviamo, a 60-foot mezzanine mixology bar, as well as Italian fare by Princi and a free show, you'll never have to leave. But if you must, don't forget to stop at the Roastery's 'scoop bar', offering 14 rotating roasts, to take some of the experience home with you.

No. 82

MON-THU.	7:00am - 11:00pm
FRI.	7:00am - 12:00am
SAT.	8:00am - 12:00am
SUN.	8:00am - 10:00pm

First opened 2018
Roaster Starbucks Reserve
Machine Victoria Arduino Black Eagle, 3 groups
Grinder Nuova Simonelli Mythos One

Espresso	$4.50
Cappuccino	$6.00 / $6.50
Latte	$6.00 / $6.50

(212) 691-0531
www.starbucksreserve.com
Subway L (8th Ave)

Sister locations Multiple locations

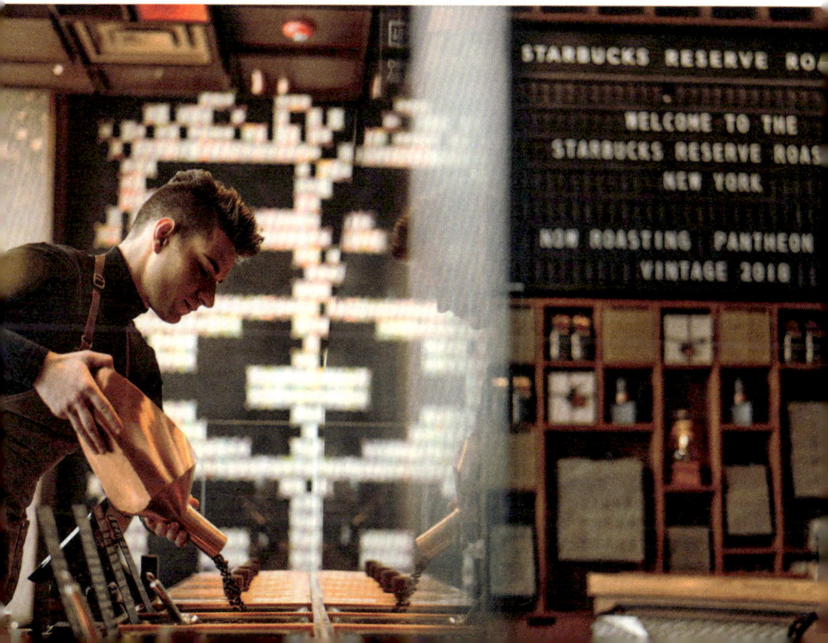

Think Coffee Hudson Yards

500 West 30th Street, Manhattan, NY 10001 | **Chelsea**

Think's consistent high quality continues in this Chelsea outpost, but the setting is unusual. It's on the edge of the Hudson Yards development, and the entrance to the Holland Tunnel isn't far away. But Think makes its own charm with a smallish, colourful interior with nice glass panelling, a friendly crew, and excellent coffee; check out their killer drip and multitude of well-crafted espresso-based drinks. With the Abington Towers apartment building nearby, and the High Line just a few minutes away, Think Coffee Chelsea is proving to be a popular spot.

www.thinkcoffee.com
Subway 7 (34th St - Hudson Yards)

Sister locations Multiple locations

MON-FRI. 6:30am - 8:00pm
SAT-SUN. 8:00am - 8:00pm

First opened 2015
Roaster Think Coffee
Machine Synesso Cyncra, 3 groups
Grinder Mazzer Luigi Super Jolly, Mahlkönig Guatemala

Espresso	$3.25
Cappuccino	$4.50
Latte	$4.50

No. 83

Underline Coffee

511 West 20th Street, Manhattan, NY 10011 | **Chelsea**

The 'line' they refer to in the title of this cool, artisan shop is of course the High Line; the beautiful elevated park that runs over this great little cafe. Classic tunes play throughout this chilled but serious coffee shop, as their handsome menus dutifully describe and explain the plenitude of offers they have on the bar. They use Apes & Peacocks for house-made speciality drinks and keep a slow bar going with single origins made to order, with both a blend and seasonal option available for espresso too.

(929) 263-4354
www.apesandpeacocks.com
Subway C, E (23rd St) or A (14th St)

MON.	7:00am - 5:00pm
TUE-SAT.	7:00am - 6:00pm
SUN.	8:00am - 5:00pm

First opened 2014
Roaster Apes & Peacocks
Machine Kees van der Westen Mirage Idrocompresso, 2 groups
Grinder Compak F10

Espresso	$3.25
Cappuccino	$4.00
Latte	$4.50

No. 84

Variety Coffee Roasters Chelsea

261 7th Avenue, Manhattan, NY 10001 | **Chelsea**

A large neon sign provides a great welcome to this Manhattan branch of Variety, and the interior is truly superb with beautifully designed tile floors, seating along the walls, and on-trend lighting. Whether meeting up with friends or using the space as your new favorite study stop, its versatile interior makes this new location the perfect spot for everyone. Enjoy a delicious cup of single-origin, ethically sourced coffee, which is roasted locally. These roasts are on-sale in store, so you can certainly take your beans to-go and brew at home! From its origins in laid-back Bushwick, Variety Coffee is very welcome in the fast-paced Manhattan coffee scene.

(917) 409-0106
www.varietycoffeeroasters.com
Subway 1, 2 (23rd St)

MON-SUN. 7:00am - 9:00pm

First opened 2017
Roaster Variety Coffee Roasters
Machine La Marzocco Linea PB ABR, 3 groups
Grinder Mahlkönig Peak

Espresso	$3.00
Cappuccino	$4.00
Latte	$4.50

Sister locations Williamsburg / Greenpoint / Bushwick / Upper East Side

No. 85

Yanni's Coffee

96 7th Avenue, Manhattan, NY 10011 | **Chelsea**

Yanni's celebrates the best of NY boroughs: a location in the heart of Chelsea, beans from Brooklyn-based Sey Coffee and a Queens native for a namesake. Inspired by family-owned beachside cafes from summer holidays in Greece, owner Yanni ditched his corporate job to open his own space, providing the Greek hospitality of his roots while celebrating his now home city. Chances are you'll catch the man himself pulling perfect shots behind the La Marzocco, clearing your cup and watching over house-baked cookies, his own personal recipe, crisping in the back oven.

(646) 833-7333
Subway L (8th Ave)

MON-FRI.	7:00am - 6:30pm
SAT.	8:00am - 6:00pm
SUN.	8:00am - 5:00pm

First opened 2018
Roaster Sey Coffee Roasters
Machine La Marzocco Linea PB, 2 groups
Grinder Mahlkönig Peak x2

Espresso	$3.00
Cappuccino	$4.00
Latte	$4.25

No. 86

Photo: Ben Hider

Midtown is fast-paced, bustling and one of the greatest commercial centers in the world. The Empire State Building, The New York Public Library, MoMA and the core of New York's theater district - including the bright lights of Times Square - can all be found in Midtown. This area is also home to the small and elegant Gramercy, a quiet neighborhood with the private, preserved Gramercy Park at its center: a lovely reminder of New York's Victorian history.

Midtown & Gramercy

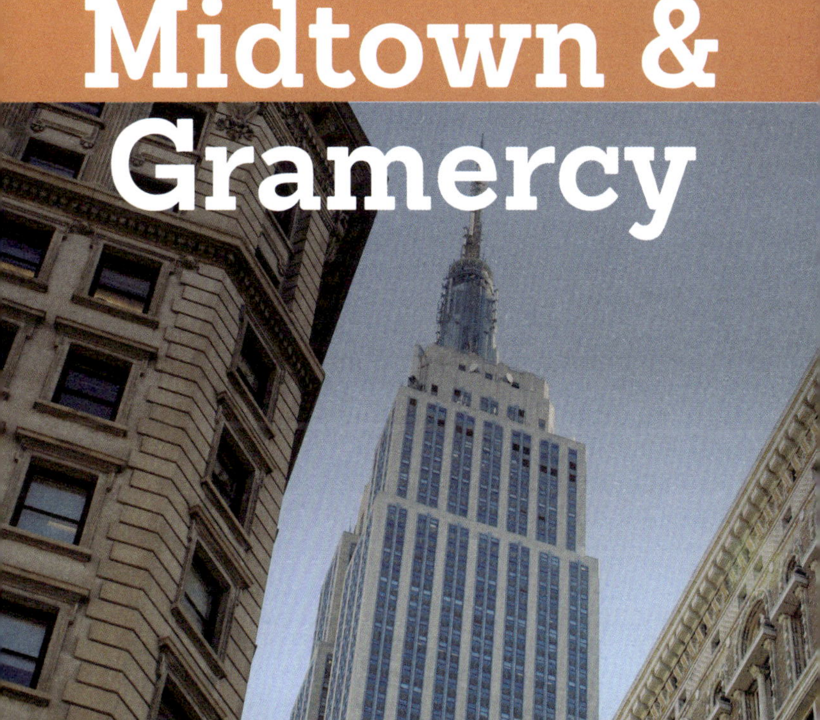

REMI Flower & Coffee. Photo: Ben Hider

Birch Coffee Flatiron

21 East 27th Street, Manhattan, NY 10016 | **Flatiron District**

Birch Coffee has made a cozy home at this end of 27th Street, with its assertively charming belief that coffee can and should bring people together. The shop has an 'Ignition Initiative' with its collection of conversation starters that they suggest people enjoy with a neighbor. Their deeply satisfying own blend coffees make for lovely treats to share with old and new friends alike.

(212) 686-1444
www.birchcoffee.com
Subway N, Q, R, W (28th St)

Sister locations Multiple locations

MON-FRI. 7:00am - 8:00pm
SAT-SUN. 8:00am - 8:00pm

First opened 2009
Roaster Birch Coffee
Machine La Marzocco Strada, 2 groups x2
Grinder Mazzer Luigi Robur

Espresso	$3.25
Cappuccino	$4.25
Latte	$4.50

Bluestone Lane Flatiron District

902 Broadway, Manhattan, NY 10010 | **Flatiron District**

This unique Bluestone Lane location pairs a full-service cafe experience with an on-demand multi-level workspace in collaboration with WeWork's newest concept in the heart of Flatiron, Made by We. The innovative space is born out of a 'community-minded' vision, combining the benefits of a collaborative and creative workspace with the escapism fostered by Bluestone's unique cafe experience. Sky-high walls are a patchwork of vintage posters and surfboards, as well as Bluestone's Brunch Club merch for avid followers of this ever-evolving cafe turned lifestyle brand.

Counter seating is available along the floor to ceiling windows looking out to bustling Broadway Ave for those grabbing a quick Sando and coffee, but if you want to hang around longer or pull out a laptop, you'll have to pay for your seat. As is the case in all branches of this Aussie-inspired gem, the flat white reigns supreme, expertly pulled with Bluestone's signature Maverick espresso blend and rich with notes of cocoa, clove, and honeycomb. But if you're feeling more indulgent, then pair your espresso with ice cream and opt for the affogato. Honestly, we'll take a Bluestone coffee any way we can get it!

No. 88

MON-FRI. 7:00am - 7:00pm
SAT-SUN. 8:00am - 6:00pm

First opened 2019
Roaster Bluestone Lane
Machine La Marzocco Linea PB, 3 groups
Grinder Mazzer Luigi Robur E,
Mahlkönig EK 43

Espresso $3.00
Cappuccino $4.00
Latte $4.00

(718) 374-6858
bluestonelane.com
Subway 4, 6 (23rd St)

Sister locations Multiple locations

Brooklyn Roasting Company Flatiron District

50 West 23rd Street, Manhattan, NY 10010 | **Flatiron District**

While Brooklyn's flagship Navy Yard roastery/cafe embraces its industrial origins, this Flatiron space is much more Manhattan-slick, with checked floor tiles and soothing cream paint on the walls and ceiling. It's a big place, and needs to be: Brooklyn's well-deserved reputation for great coffee (single-origin drip is always sensational) and good food draws in crowds so big they need a rope barrier to keep them orderly. There's a nice mix of office workers and hipster aficionados here.

(718) 412-0080
www.brooklynroasting.com
Subway F, M (23rd St)

Sister locations Multiple locations

MON-FRI. 7:00am - 7:00pm
SAT. 8:00am - 6:00pm
SUN. Closed

First opened 2015
Roaster Brooklyn Roasting Company
Machine La Marzocco GB5, 2 groups
Grinder Nuova Simonelli Mythos One Clima Pro

Espresso	$2.75
Cappuccino	$4.00
Latte	$4.50

No. 89

Café Grumpy Grand Central Terminal

89 East 42nd Street, Manhattan, NY 10017 | **Midtown East**

Café Grumpy's Grand Central outlet has loads of competitors for your brew-time buck, but it offers something special: a small, attractive space with a window onto Lexington Avenue. It feels like a real cafe rather than a mass-transit pit stop. Despite the size you may have luck getting a seat, because so much of the trade is takeout. Carry your beautifully crafted latte to a table and sit down to read The New Yorker, or just look out the window. GCT is all hustle and bustle, but Grumpy is all sip and chill.

(212) 661-2198
cafegrumpy.com
Subway S, 4, 5, 6, 7 (Grand Central - 42nd St)

Sister locations Multiple locations

MON-FRI. 6:00am - 8:00pm
SAT-SUN. 7:00am - 8:00pm

First opened 2014
Roaster Café Grumpy
Machine Synesso MVP Hydra, 2 groups x2
Grinder Nuova Simonelli Mythos

Espresso	$3.75
Cappuccino	$4.50
Latte	$5.00

No. 90

Citizens of Gramercy

362 2nd Avenue, Manhattan, NY 10010 | **Gramercy**

Citizens of Gramercy embodies a 'new' New York brand of casual daytime excellence, where getting a healthy, luxurious meal and enjoying first-rate coffee isn't mutually exclusive. On their all-day menu, stunningly green avocado toast is served with magenta pickled onions and swooshes of beetroot hummus. Laid perfectly alongside are jade coffee cups filled to the brim with perfectly executed latte art that screams to be photographed. Think pink with frozé all day or coffee enthusiasts can opt for the creamy, rich nitro cold-brew martini. The color scheme is rounded out with a glowing pink neon sign and luscious green plant-life scattered throughout the cafe. Coincidence? I think not. Citizens of Instagram, meet your match.

(212) 262-5492
citizens.coffee
Subway L (3rd Ave)

MON-FRI.	7:30am - 6:00pm
SAT-SUN.	8:00am - 6:00pm

First opened 2018
Roaster Partners Coffee
Machine La Marzocco Linea, 2 groups
Grinder Mazzer Luigi Robur

Espresso	$3.50
Cappuccino	$4.50
Latte	$4.75

Sister locations Citizens of Chelsea

No. 91

Culture 36

247 West 36th Street, Manhattan, NY 10018 | **Garment District**

Photo: Albert Cheung

The second Garment District outpost of Culture Espresso is true to its name: espresso and its milky offspring are front and center. You won't be disappointed, because the baristas know what they're doing with their gleaming La Marzocco. The Heart blend is bright and bracing, easily good enough to drink without sugar. There's an original ceiling high overhead and one big table offering the bulk of the seating in the spacious room. They bake their own delicious chocolate chip cookies, and once you've had one, you'll keep coming back for more.

(646) 861-3553
www.cultureespresso.com
Subway A, C, E (34th St - Penn Station)

MON-FRI. 7:00am - 7:00pm
SAT-SUN. 8:00am - 7:00pm

First opened 2014
Roaster Heart Coffee Roasters
Machine La Marzocco Strada AV, 3 groups
Grinder Mazzer Luigi Robur E, Mahlkönig EK 43, Mahlkönig K30 Twin

Espresso $3.50
Cappuccino $4.25
Latte $4.75

Sister locations Culture 307 / Culture Espresso

No. 92

Culture 307

307 West 38th Street, Manhattan, NY 10018 | **Garment District**

Nestled between towering office buildings, this small but mighty cafe is the third edition of Midtown-based Culture espresso. Two-top tables and bench seating bring chatting pairs and laptop dwellers together to enjoy deep caramel and buttery smooth espresso-based brews. The bright, airy space is perfectly petite and, with its colossal floor to ceiling windows, is a sublime spot to watch the bustling streets of Midtown. Come here to unwind and recharge, coffee in one hand, legendary cookie in the other.

(646) 864-1963
www.cultureespresso.com
Subway A, C, E (34th St - Penn Stn) or F, N, Q, R, W (Times Sq - 42nd St)

MON-FRI. 7:00am - 7:00pm
SAT-SUN. 8:00am - 7:00pm

First opened 2017
Roaster Heart Coffee Roasters
Machine La Marzocco Strada MP, 3 groups
Grinder Mazzer Luigi Robur E

Espresso $3.50
Cappuccino $4.25
Latte $4.75

Sister locations Culture 36 / Culture Espresso

No. 93

Culture Espresso

TOP 40

72 West 38th Street, Manhattan, NY 10018 | **Midtown West**

Years ago, Culture was pretty much the only place to get great coffee near 42nd Street. Even though that's no longer the case, Culture's relaxed California-tinged atmosphere - despite constant foot-traffic - makes it stand out. Besides Stumptown's impossibly creamy, must-try nitro cold-brew on draught, the beans are from the excellent Heart Coffee Roasters of Portland.
The baristas know what they're doing here, and you can't go wrong, whether you order an espresso, macchiato, or flat white. There's just enough space to sit down and relax, as you watch Midtown race by.

(212) 302-0200
www.cultureespresso.com
Subway B, D, F, M (42nd St - Bryant Park)

MON-FRI. 7:00am - 7:00pm
SAT-SUN. 8:00am - 7:00pm

First opened 2009
Roaster Heart Coffee Roasters
Machine La Marzocco Strada AV, 3 groups
Grinder Mazzer Luigi Robur E, Mahlkönig EK 43

Espresso $3.50
Cappuccino $4.25
Latte $4.75

Sister locations Culture 36 / Culture 307

No. 94

Devoción Flatiron District

25 East 20th Street, Manhattan, NY 10003 | **Flatiron District**

Devoción knows how to choose a space. Winningly open and flooded with light, their introduction to Manhattan still manages to foster the chill and earthy environment inspired by Colombia, with all the familiar tropes of their Brooklyn locations. That means skylights, Colombian plant life, and leather couches to sink deep into. Their focus on sustainability and ethics enrich the entire supply chain while their obsession with finding the finest coffee varieties across Colombia results in the best ancestral varieties from 400 micro-lots. These arrive via FedEx, for the freshest, most complex selection of coffee which they say still breathes the mist of the Colombian campo. Come and enjoy this Colombian coffee paradise.

(718) 285-6180
www.devocion.com
Subway 4, 6 (23rd St)

MON-FRI. 7:00am - 7:00pm
SAT-SUN. 8:00am - 7:00pm

First opened 2018
Roaster Devoción
Machine Slayer Espresso, 3 groups
Grinder Ceado E37K

Espresso $3.50
Cappuccino $4.50
Latte $5.00

Sister locations Williamsburg / Downtown Brooklyn

No. 95

Dr Smood

1151 Broadway, Manhattan, NY 10001 | **Midtown West**

'Smart food for a good mood.' That is the slogan for Dr Smood, a stylish venue situated near Madison Square Park. With its sleek interior aesthetic that includes an exposed brick wall, comfortable seating, WiFi, and charging ports a-plenty, Dr Smood is a popular hub for health-conscious millennials on a lunchbreak. In terms of their beverage servings, the brew never disappoints - and if you're in the mood for something a little fruity, their extensive own brand juice catalogue has you covered too. Dr Smood is making healthy waves in the New York coffee scene, and we are loving it!

(646) 7131-380
drsmood.com
Subway N, Q, R, W (28th St)

MON-FRI. 7:00am - 7:00pm
SAT-SUN. 9:00am - 7:00pm

First opened 2017
Roaster Dr Smood
Machine La Marzocco Linea PB, 3 groups
Grinder La Marzocco Swift

Espresso $3.00
Cappuccino $5.50
Latte $5.50

Sister locations Multiple locations

Felix Roasting Co.

450 Park Avenue South, Manhattan, NY 10016 | **Murray Hill**

Felix Roasting Co. is a pastel palace which leaves you lost in space and time. The opulent and luxurious world of floral booth seating, custom starburst terrazzo floors, hand-drawn arabica plant wallpaper, and historical iconography is thoroughly transportive. It's an artisanal dream: cups are handmade, sugar packets hand-drawn and a cashew-almond-pepita milk alternative is made in house. Combine all of this with their precise and fresh food program featuring cult favorite Supermoon's extravagant pastries and you have the perfect foundation for an immersive and ritualistic experience of coffee. Vibrant coffees are hand-selected from all over the world through consideration of seasonality and thoughtful partnerships and then carefully roasted in Texas, respecting the flavor and uniqueness of their origins.

If you order the s'mores latte, expect a show as baristas smoke the decadent drink inside a giant bell jar and garnish it with a scorched house-made salted caramel marshmallow. Looking around and watching people commune over perfectly prepared coffee - eyes closed with that first sip and opened to exceptional design and visual storytelling - is the pure and simple joy of Felix.

No. 97

MON-THU.	7:00am - 6:00pm
FRI.	7:00am - 8:00pm
SAT.	8:00am - 8:00pm
SUN.	8:00am - 6:00pm

decaf

First opened 2018
Roaster Felix Roasting Co.
Machine Modbar AV, 2 groups, La Marzocco Linea PB, 2 groups
Grinder Mazzer Luigi Kold, Mahlkönig EK 43

Espresso	$3.50
Cappuccino	$4.25
Latte	$4.50

felixroastingco.com
Subway 6 (28th St)

FIKA Tower & Bakery

824 10th Avenue, Manhattan, NY 10019 | **Hell's Kitchen**

FIKA's 10th Avenue space is one of its best, with tall ceilings, white walls, copious light from the front windows and skylight, and discreet but distinctive decorative touches. This is a place to come and eat gorgeous Swedish-inspired food, with large platters a specialty. Of course, being Swedish, it does not neglect the sweet stuff either. There is a touch of berry sweetness in their well-made espresso, crafted with care and served with a smile. A great place to come after exploring the pier, just two blocks away.

(646) 490-7650
www.fikanyc.com
Subway 1, A, B, C, D (59th St - Columbus Circle)

Sister locations Multiple locations

MON-FRI. 7:00am - 7:00pm
SAT-SUN. 9:00am - 7:00pm

First opened 2014
Roaster Unique Coffee Roasters
Machine Synesso Cyncra, 3 groups
Grinder Compak

Espresso	$3.00
Cappuccino	$4.75
Latte	$5.00

No. 98

For Five Coffee Roasters

117 46th Street, Manhattan, NY 10036 | **Midtown West**

Beginning as a micro-roastery opened by two best friends in Queens, For Five is fast becoming an institution to meet your every caffeine-based dream. Their mantra is 'specialty coffee by New Yorkers for New Yorkers'; be they rushing to the office craving a cappuccino and croissant, or a freelancer with time to spare relaxing with a single-origin pour over and house-made salad. The incredible integrity and care in each preparation from their bright cold brew to their hand whisked matcha is what makes them truly stand out. The only problem at For Five is deciding what to order. Luckily, the line out the door supplies ample time for decision making!

(347) 619-3194
forfivecoffee.com
Subway D, F, M (47-50th St - Rockefeller Center)

MON-FRI.	7:00am - 7:00pm
SAT.	9:00am - 4:00pm
SUN.	Closed

First opened 2016
Roaster For Five Coffee Roasters
Machine Sanremo Opera, 2 groups, Modbar, 2 groups
Grinder Mahlkönig EK 43

Espresso	$3.25
Cappuccino	$4.25
Latte	$4.75

Sister locations Financial District / Gossip powered by For Five

No. 99

Frisson Espresso Hell's Kitchen

326 West 47th Street, Manhattan, NY 10036 | **Hell's Kitchen**

Owners Tulian Sanchez and Robert Melo have been friends since they were five, so it's not surprising that they work together well in running this peachy Hell's Kitchen espresso spot. The place, which seats around sixteen people, can be jumping any time of day with a clientele they describe as 'a little bit of everything'. Coffee is well made using beans from Dallis Bros. in Long Island City, and latte art is beautiful. Try to bag a table if you can and just sit back and enjoy the show.

(646) 850-3928
www.frissonespresso.com
Subway 1, 2, A, C, E (50th St) or N, Q, R, W (49th St)

Sister locations East Village

MON-FRI.	7:00am - 8:00pm
SAT.	8:00am - 8:00pm
SUN.	8:00am - 7:00pm

First opened 2014
Roaster Dallis Bros. Coffee
Machine Synesso Cyncra, 3 groups
Grinder Compak E10

Espresso	$3.25
Cappuccino	$4.25
Latte	$4.75

No. **100**

Gasoline Alley Coffee Flatiron

24 East 23rd Street, Manhattan, NY 10010 | **Flatiron District**

Gasoline Alley always wins with its memorable coffee, and this snug Flatiron venue is no different. Conveniently placed for those needing to power up on their way to work, the service is as friendly and efficient as you'd expect from the guys at Gasoline Alley. Beans are from Intelligentsia and brewed with skill across the board. There's a bit of seating too, with a good view across 23rd Street of Madison Square Park.

(212) 933-0113
www.gasolinealleycoffee.com
Subway N, Q, R, W (23rd St) or 4, 6 (23rd St)

Sister locations Noho / Soho / West Village

MON-FRI.	7:00am - 7:00pm
SAT.	8:00am - 6:00pm
SUN.	8:00am - 5:00pm

First opened 2016
Roaster Intelligentsia Coffee
Machine La Marzocco GB5, 3 groups
Grinder Mazzer Luigi Robur E

Espresso	$3.00
Cappuccino	$4.25
Latte	$4.50

No. 101

Gotham Coffee Roasters

23 West 19th Street, Manhattan, NY 10011 | **Flatiron District**

This lively Flatiron shop is a bustling weekday spot that brings in the work crowd from the surrounding neighborhood, and we can see why. Pulling shots of fragrant single origin coffees, the skilled baristas will make you a drink to remember whether you have your espresso with silky milk or straight up. Their regular rotation of new coffees sourced from across the globe and roasted in Brooklyn keeps the offer interesting, with something new and exciting to try every time you visit. Make sure to grab a bag while you're there and recreate your favorite brews at home.

(212) 255-2972
www.gothamroasters.com
Subway N, Q, R, W (East 23rd St)
or F, M, L (14th St)

MON-FRI. 7:00am - 7:00pm
SAT-SUN. 8:30am - 6:30pm

First opened 2017
Roaster Gotham Coffee Roasters
Machine La Marzocco Linea PB EE, 2 groups
Grinder Mahlkönig Peak, Mahlkönig EK 43

Espresso $3.50
Cappuccino $4.50
Latte $4.75

No. 102

Gregorys Coffee Gramercy

327 Park Avenue South, Manhattan, NY 10010 | **Gramercy**

This branch of Gregorys is one of the most popular places in the area among office workers who want conviviality with their coffee: the tables lining the long, narrow room are often full, and it's not just with those tapping on a keyboard. It's a very welcoming space, nicely decorated with a combination of dark colors and bright lighting, and the customary Gregorys offerings of both food and drink keep up the company's high standards. Gregorys own in-house baked goods are exceptional, and a wide range of non-espresso brews makes coffee selection a challenging pleasure.

(212) 979-8600
www.gregoryscoffee.com
Subway 4, 6 (23rd St)

Sister locations Multiple locations

MON-FRI. 6:00am - 8:00pm
SAT. 6:00am - 7:00pm
SUN. 7:00am - 7:00pm

First opened 2006
Roaster Gregorys Coffee
Machine La Marzocco Linea PB, 3 groups
Grinder Mazzer Luigi Kold

Espresso $3.00
Cappuccino $4.00
Latte $4.65

No. 103

Ground Central Coffee Company 2nd Avenue

800 2nd Avenue, Manhattan, NY 10013 | **Midtown East**

This small branch of Ground Central, the company's second, maintains a steady buzz thanks to two huge nearby suppliers of thirsty workers: Grand Central Station and the UN. It's not surprising that customers choose Ground Central, with coffee this good pouring steadily out of their machines. Single-origin drip and pour over are outstanding, from a changing range. The espresso-based drinks feature latte art that could easily win professional competitions. No wonder Ground Central is almost as busy as Grand Central.

(646) 861-0015
www.ground-central.com
Subway S, 4, 5, 6, 7 (Grand Central - 42nd St)

MON-FRI. 6:30am - 7:00pm
SAT-SUN. 7:00am - 5:00pm

First opened 2014
Roaster La Colombe Coffee Roasters
Machine La Marzocco FB80
Grinder Mazzer Luigi Robur E

Espresso $3.10
Cappuccino $4.10
Latte $4.25

Sister locations Financial District / Midtown East / Midtown West

No. 104

Ground Central Coffee Company

52nd Street 155 East 52nd Street, Manhattan, NY 10017 | **Midtown East**

This original branch of Ground Central feels more like a European-style cafe than a contemporary-style coffee place. It's sleek and elegant, and the prominence given to their serious sandwiches and enticing baked goods makes it clear that food plays a major role. Swap your coffee for a cocktail later in the day. A collection of vinyl discs lines a front wall, and the soundtrack favors timeless rock 'n' roll classics. The baristas rock their three-group La Marzocco, too, but don't neglect the single-origin drip brews.

(646) 964-4438
www.ground-central.com
Subway E, M (Lexington Ave - 53rd St)

Sister locations Midtown East / Financial District / Midtown West

MON-FRI. 6:30am - 9:00pm
SAT-SUN. 9:00am - 6:00pm

First opened 2014
Roaster La Colombe Coffee Roasters
Machine La Marzocco Linea, 3 groups
Grinder Mazzer Luigi Robur E

Espresso	$3.10
Cappuccino	$4.10
Latte	$4.25

No. 105

Hole in the Wall Murray Hill

626 1st Avenue, Manhattan, NY 10016 | **Murray Hill**

The owners may have to come up with a change of name for their newest location. Nestled at the base of the American Copper Buildings, this daytime cafe/nighttime restaurant flaunts 28-foot glass walls on three sides, allowing lovely views out to the east river. Flat whites and flat white plates topped with artfully displayed food greet tables with a smile, as an elevated all-day brunch menu from açaí bowls to pulled pork benedict gives way to a sophisticated seasonal dinner menu. Novo beans go perfectly with skillfully frothed milk while a delicate batch brew is best enjoyed as it comes. Enjoy al-fresco, or just at a table really close to the glass wall.

www.holeinthewallnyc.com
Subway 4, 6 (33rd St)

MON-SUN. 7:00am - 11:00pm

First opened 2019
Roaster Novo Coffee
Machine Synesso MVP Hydra, 3 groups
Grinder Mazzer Luigi

Espresso	$3.25
Cappuccino	$4.25
Latte	$4.75

Sister locations Financial District / Midtown

No. 106

Irving Farm New York Gramercy

71 Irving Place, Manhattan, NY 10003 | **Gramercy**

Settled at the bottom of a brownstone on quiet Irving Place, Irving Farm is a New York City institution. The street may be serene, but step inside to find a cafe bustling with energy. There is a constant stream of people moving in and out of this cozy cafe, which can be a bit snug in terms of seating, but that is part of its charming atmosphere. The lights are low, the baristas are pros, and their coffee, which is roasted at their Hudson Valley roastery, is expertly brewed.

(212) 206-0707
irvingfarm.com
Subway N, Q, R, W, 4, 5, 6, L (14th St - Union Sq)

Sister locations Multiple locations

MON-FRI. 7:00am - 8:00pm
SAT-SUN. 8:00am - 8:00pm

First opened 1996
Roaster Irving Farm New York
Machine La Marzocco Linea AV, 2 groups
Grinder Nuova Simonelli Mythos Clima Pro

Espresso	$3.25
Cappuccino	$4.50
Latte	$4.75

No. **107**

Irving Farm New York Midtown East

135 East 50th Street, Manhattan, NY 10022 | **Midtown East**

This Irving Farm spot in Midtown East truly outdoes itself in all areas; quality, aesthetic, and customer service. Friendly baristas execute their craft with knowledge and care, pulling consistently great espressos and delicious cappuccinos. With its black concrete floors and burnished brass details, the shop's design is heavily influenced by the surrounding neighborhood. Additionally, the spot boasts a menu by Danielle Dillon, serving up modern comfort food. It's a place for anyone really: moms wheeling strollers, co-workers on their lunch break, or diligent students studying for midterms.

(212) 206-0707
irvingfarm.com
Subway 4, 6 (51st St) or E, M (Lexington Ave - 53rd St)

MON-FRI. 7:00am - 6:00pm
SAT-SUN. 8:00am - 6:00pm

First opened 2017
Roaster Irving Farm New York
Machine La Marzocco Linea PB, 2 groups
Grinder Nuova Simonelli Mythos One Clima Pro

Espresso	$3.25
Cappuccino	$4.50
Latte	$4.75

Sister locations Multiple locations

No. 108

Joe & The Juice Midtown East

286 Madison Avenue, Manhattan, NY 10017 | **Midtown East**

The east 40s don't suffer from a shortage of places to eat and drink, but this branch of Joe & The Juice is an extremely welcome addition to the scene. Yes, you can come and get your latte and your avocado sandwich to go and eat them at your desk. But if you want a break from the office, this is an unexpectedly pleasant place to sit and talk - well spaced tables in an attractive corner site, not to forget the upbeat Danish vibes. Espresso-based drinks are always well made, and a big cup of filter is also a great option. And then there are famous juices, for those who want fruit with their beans.

www.joejuice.com
Subway 7 (5th Ave) or 4, 5, 6, 7, S (Grand Central - 42nd St)

MON-FRI. 7:00am - 8:00pm
SAT-SUN. 8:00am - 7:00pm

First opened 2017
Roaster Joe & The Juice
Machine La Marzocco GB5 AV, 3 groups
Grinder Nuova Simonelli Mythos One

Espresso $2.70
Cappuccino $4.30
Latte $4.30

Sister locations Multiple locations

No. 109

Kahve

667 10th Avenue, Manhattan, NY 10019 | **Hell's Kitchen**

The second incarnation of Kahve is brightly modern in décor and has much more seating space than the nearby original. It's a very good place to settle in for working, though the seats in the window make a good place for people-watching. In addition to the signature Kahve offerings of brewed coffee, espresso-based drinks, and indulgent latte tweaks, this branch serves nitro-brew from a tap on the counter. The baristas know their business, and they know how to smile, a winning combination from this rising star of New York's coffee scene.

(646) 649-4503
www.kahvenyc.com
Subway A, C, E (50th St)

Sister locations Hell's Kitchen

MON-TUE. 7:00am - 8:00pm
WED-FRI. 7:00am - 10:00pm
SAT. 7:30am - 10:00pm
SUN. 8:00am - 8:00pm

First opened 2016
Roaster Kahve
Machine Nuova Simonelli Aurelia, 3 groups
Grinder Nuova Simonelli MDX

Espresso $2.50
Cappuccino $3.85
Latte $4.65

No. 110

Le Café Coffee

7 East 14th Street, Manhattan, NY 10003 | **Gramercy**

Situated in the middle of the always hectic 14th Street, Le Café Coffee is an oasis from the Manhattan mayhem. It's small, but never too crowded, making it the perfect spot to take a seat and relax amidst the outside chaos. The service is refreshingly friendly, the conversation personalized as they prepare your order. They serve espresso-based beverages as well as drip alongside a small menu of fresh sandwiches. Additionally, there is a seasonal menu of specialty beverages, and their matcha latte is especially of note.

(212) 365-1060
www.lecafecoffee.com
Subway 4, 5,6, N, Q, R, W, L (14th St - Union Sq)

MON-THU. 7:00am - 8:30pm
FRI. 7:00am - 9:00pm
SAT. 8:00am - 9:00pm
SUN. 8:00am - 8:00pm

First opened 2013
Roaster La Colombe Coffee Roasters
Machine La Marzocco GB5, 2 groups
Grinder Mazzer Luigi

Espresso $3.25
Cappuccino $4.25
Latte $4.50

Sister locations Union Sq / Midtown East / Midtown West / Flatiron

No. 111

Little Collins

667 Lexington Avenue, Manhattan, NY 10022 | **Midtown East**

Australian-influenced Little Collins is the civilized coffee shop Midtown East has always needed but didn't have until 2013. Focused, friendly baristas in old-fashioned uniforms work diligently and quickly to serve a constant stream of business people and yogis. If you're able to snag a stool, the staff make you feel at home, pouring you tap water without being asked to do so. The espresso, strong and delicious, comes with a tiny almond cookie, a nice touch. Single-origin pour overs are made with a Modbar contraption which heats and pours the water - it's like having a robot hand-pour your coffee.

(212) 308-1969
www.littlecollinsnyc.com
Subway E, M (Lexington Ave - 53rd St)

MON-FRI. 7:00am - 5:00pm
SAT-SUN. 8:00am - 4:00pm

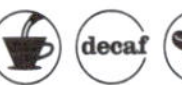

First opened 2013
Roaster Counter Culture Coffee
Machine Modbar, 2 groups
Grinder Mahlkönig EK 43,
Nuova Simonelli Mythos One Clima Pro

Espresso	$3.75
Cappuccino	$4.75
Latte	$4.75

No. 112

Ninth Street Espresso Midtown East

109 East 56th Street, Manhattan, NY 10022 | **Midtown East**

The Ninth Street Espresso menu boasts just four options, none of which are 'cappuccino' or latte' - instead, simply 'espresso with milk'. This minimalist touch is one of several ways it conveys it's serious about espresso, and the strong, viscous shots back that up. The timeless, black-and-white-tiled space, inside the swanky Lombardy hotel, has a few stools, but is more suited to the droves of businesspeople who line up to throw back a shot. If you can avoid feeling like a philistine in comparison, order the smooth, sweet cold brew; it may be the best in the city.

(646) 861-1440
www.ninthstreetespresso.com
Subway E, M (Lexington Ave - 53rd St)

Sister locations Multiple locations

MON-FRI. 7:00am - 7:00pm
SAT-SUN. 8:00am - 3:00pm

First opened 2013
Roaster Ninth Street Roasting
Machine La Marzocco GB5 EE, 2 groups
Grinder Mahlkönig EK 43

Espresso	$3.50
Cappuccino	$4.50
Latte	$4.50

No. 113

Optimistic Cafe

260 West 39th Street, Manhattan, NY 10018 | **Garment District**

This Midtown shop, nestled on 39th Street just around the corner from the Port Authority Terminal, is a refreshing little cafe with a rustic interior, highlighted by a lush wall of live greenery. Cheerful baristas pull shots of Counter Culture espresso on their bright yellow Slayer, while their in-house chef serves up made-to-order sandwiches and breakfast dishes. If you need a place to get away from the hustle and bustle of Midtown, this is the perfect place to sit down, have a bite and a coffee, and perhaps get a bit more optimistic about your day (or life) in the city that never sleeps.

(646) 998-3970
optimisticcafe.com
Subway 7, N, Q, R, W (Times Sq - 42nd St)

MON-SUN. 7:00am - 7:00pm

First opened 2017
Roaster Counter Culture Coffee
Machine Slayer Espresso, 3 groups
Grinder Mahlkönig EKK 43, Nuova Simonelli Mythos One

Espresso	$3.25
Cappuccino	$4.00
Latte	$4.50

Sister locations Milk and Honey Café

No. 114

Orens Coffee Times Square

1440 Broadway, Manhattan, NY 10018 | **Midtown West**

Orens does a brisk business for good reasons: the coffee is solid and the store's well run. At this branch, nearly everyone seems to come in for something to go. Single-origin brews, using beans bought directly from the producers, are the obvious choice for drinking on the move.

This branch, one of Orens eight locations in New York, is right on the doorstep of the tourist-and-traffic magnet that is Times Square and 42nd Street, a welcome addition to this busy area.

(212) 348-5400
www.orenscoffee.com
Subway B, D, F, M (42nd St - Bryant Park) or N, Q, R, W (Times Sq - 42nd St)

Sister locations Multiple locations

MON-FRI.	7:00am - 7:00pm
SAT-SUN.	Closed

First opened 2010
Roaster Orens Coffee
Machine La Marzocco GB5, 2 groups
Grinder Mazzer Luigi Robur E, Mahlkönig Guatemala Lab

Espresso	$3.00
Cappuccino	$4.00
Latte	$4.00

Paper Coffee

44 West 29th Street, Manhattan, NY 10001 | **Midtown West**

This beautiful cafe in the hotel entryway of MADE Hotel celebrates the simple joy of a morning coffee and newspaper. While the aesthetics alone may impress, Paper's food and beverage program are equally accomplished thanks to its partnership with MADE's Ferris restaurant. Here they rotate the house blend of Regalia Coffee with a focus on seasonality, while continuing to feature other quality guest roasters who catch their attention. The espresso on offer for our visit was a Colombian and naturally processed Ethiopian blend - rich in cocoa with a berry crispness. Grab a paper, sip from your handmade mug at a raw wood table, and get analog!

(212) 213-4429
www.madehotels.com/eat-drink
Subway 1, 2, 3 (Penn Station - 134th St)

MON-SUN. 7:00am - 5:00pm

First opened 2017
Roaster Paper Coffee
Machine La Marzocco Linea PB, 2 groups
Grinder Mahlkönig EK 43

Espresso	$3.50
Cappuccino	$4.50
Latte	$5.00

No. **116**

Pennylane Coffee

305 East 45th Street, Manhattan, NY 10017 | **Midtown East**

The first thing that strikes you about Pennylane is the spacious interior. It is sleekly designed, with a windowed wall front that opens up in the summer, while subtle, mellow rock music plays in the background. This is a space where you could happily hang out all day. But not only hitting the design mark, Pennylane delivers delicious, smooth coffee with distinctive flavor, served up by baristas who really know their craft. And, once you're sufficiently caffeinated, you can even switch over to one of the wines or craft beers on offer and enjoy one of their delicious sandwiches.

(917) 797-5133
Subway 4, 5, 6, 7, S (Grand Central - 42nd St)

MON-FRI. 7:00am - 6:30pm
SAT-SUN. 8:00am - 2:00pm

First opened 2013
Roaster Heart Coffee Roasters, Sweetleaf Coffee Roasters, The Coffee Collective
Machine La Marzocco Strada EP, 3 groups
Grinder Mazzer Luigi x2

Espresso $3.25
Cappuccino $4.25
Latte $4.75

No. 117

Perk Kafe

162 East 37th Street, Manhattan, NY 10016 | **Murray Hill**

The sedate precincts of Murray Hill are probably not the first place you'd think of as the location for a seriously distinguished, extremely laid-back coffee destination. But that's what you get in Perk Kafe. It's not a big place, and can get crowded, but it's worth a visit for the quality of the coffee alone. Beans from Stumptown get the royal treatment, including various non-espresso alternatives if you're a single-origin lover. Latte art is exemplary, and the welcome is friendly. A great place in an unexpected area.

(212) 686-7375
perkkafe.com
Subway 4, 6 (33rd St)

MON-SUN. 8:00am - 7:00pm

First opened 2013
Roaster Stumptown Coffee Roasters
Machine La Marzocco Linea, 2 groups
Grinder Mazzer Luigi Super Jolly, Mazzer Luigi Kony

Espresso $3.25
Cappuccino $4.25
Latte $4.50

Sister locations East Harlem

No. 118

PROOF Coffee Roasters Carmel

335 East 27th Street, Manhattan, NY 10016 | **Kips Bay**

Next time you find yourself lost in Kips Bay, and craving a pick-me-up, make sure to scurry over to PROOF. Signature pastries are served with love and ethically sourced beans, roasted in Red Hook, make for beautiful, rich coffee that packs a lot of punch. Their cold brew is especially noteworthy, and well worth deviating from the regular espresso-based drinks for, while the bright open space and tranquil surroundings are ideal for laptopping. If you're a local, opt for their monthly coffee membership for unlimited drip coffee and tea, and discounted specialty drinks. A perfect addition to the area which is somewhat lacking in restaurants, bars and cafes, PROOF is hopefully a sign of more to come!

(212) 689-1000
www.proof.coffee
Subway 4, 6 (28th St)

MON-FRI.	7:00am - 7:00pm
SAT-SUN.	9:00am - 5:00pm

First opened 2017
Roaster PROOF Coffee Roasters
Machine La Marzocco GB5, 2 groups
Grinder Mahlkönig K30 Vario Air, Anfim SCODY II

Espresso	$3.00
Cappuccino	$4.00
Latte	$4.50

Sister locations SVK / Nassau / ACP / 5th Avenue

No. 119

Ramini Espresso Bar

265 West 37th Street, Manhattan, NY 10018 | **Midtown West**

Ramini is a key player in major-league coffee. Its pretty interior has some quirky features and you can always expect an exceptionally warm welcome from coffee-obsessed baristas. The tasty baked goods, are mostly made on the premises and they also offer a superior selection of teas and fresh-squeezed juices. Liquids from the three-group Sanremo are common, but if you want a real change, go for a cup from the towering Kyoto drip apparatus, the world's slowest drip machine. An unexpected and really delightful find in Midtown.

(347) 907-0343
www.ramininyc.com
Subway A, C, E (34th St - Penn Station)

MON-FRI.	7:00am - 5:00pm
SAT.	9:00am - 1:00pm
SUN.	Closed

First opened 2012
Roaster Brooklyn Roasting Company
Machine Sanremo Café Racer, 3 groups
Grinder Mazzer Luigi Super Jolly E

Espresso	$3.00
Cappuccino	$5.75
Latte	$5.75

No. 120

REMI Flower & Coffee

906 2nd Avenue, Manhattan, NY 10017 | **Murray Hill**

The New York coffee community keeps sprouting these places with a little bit extra. Prepare for the ultimate arousal of senses when visiting this cafe/florist which, thanks to an abundance of plant life, may have the highest air quality in the NY coffee scene. Finding inspiration in their floral surroundings, baristas transform La Colombe beans into specialty drinks, including an addictive honey latte, strong with coffee and a delicate floral finish, and their now Insta-famous rose and lavender lattes, brightly colored and adorned with petals. You may have to fight some enthusiastic Grammers for a seat in this not-so-secret garden, or just grab a bouquet and coffee to go.

(646) 559-1233
www.reminyc.com
Subway 4, 6 (Lexington - 53rd St)

MON-FRI. 7:00am - 7:00pm
SAT-SUN. 8:00am - 6:00pm

First opened 2017
Roaster La Colombe Coffee Roasters
Machine La Marzocco GB5, 2 groups
Grinder Nuova Simonelli Mythos One

Espresso $3.00
Cappuccino $4.00
Latte $4.50

No. 121

REX

864 10th Avenue, Manhattan, NY 10039 | **Hell's Kitchen**

REX does its name proud, as this shop is one of the kings. It's got wonderfully prepared coffees from Counter Culture and features a slow bar with seasonal single origins that the staff will happily discuss with you. They also run an astonishingly impressive kitchen, preparing surprises such as house-cured gravlax for fresh sandwiches and impossibly delicious baked goods; the flourless chocolate brownies are one to try. It's a welcome coffee oasis in Hell's Kitchen and though small, it's got two comfy, communal tables and enough charm to make it a cozy, inviting space to visit for a refuel.

(914) 602-6367
www.rexcoffeenyc.com
Subway 1, A, B, C, D (59th St - Columbus Circle)

MON-FRI.	7:00am - 6:00pm
SAT.	8:00am - 6:00pm
SUN.	8:00am - 4:00pm

First opened 2013
Roaster Counter Culture Coffee
Machine La Marzocco Linea PB, 2 groups
Grinder Mazzer Luigi Robur, Mahlkönig EK 43

Espresso	$3.50
Cappuccino	$4.00
Latte	$4.50

No. 122

Ruby's Murray Hill

442 3rd Avenue, Manhattan, NY 10016 | **Murray Hill**

You'll spot the Murray Hill branch of Ruby's from some distance, because there's almost certain to be a crowd standing outside waiting for a table. This Midtown spot duplicates the wildly successful model of the Aussie-inspired Soho original, but in a somewhat smaller package. If you're looking for just a quick coffee, we'd recommend arriving outside mealtimes to avoid the food rush. Though even that's no guarantee of instant entry; a true testament to its popularity. If the weather is right, the iced coffee at Ruby's is a particularly tasty option.

(212) 300-4245
www.rubyscafe.com
Subway 4, 6 (33rd St)

MON-SUN.	9:00am - 10:30pm

First opened 2016
Roaster La Colombe Coffee Roasters
Machine La Marzocco GB5, 2 groups
Grinder Mazzer Luigi

Espresso	$3.50
Cappuccino	$4.00
Latte	$4.00

Sister locations Soho

No. 123

Seven Grams Caffé Flatiron

76 Madison Avenue, Manhattan, NY 10016 | **Flatiron District**

If you need to escape the office to A) caffeinate and B) stress eat some cookies, go to Seven Grams. This corner cafe with beechwood bench seating catches light between the towers of midtown with sky-high windows and even higher ceilings. Taking its name from the true Italian standard, where the perfect espresso is made from precisely seven grams of coffee, precision and order provide the foundation of this cafe. So it only makes sense that it is also a bakery, where everything is made from scratch daily after scrupulous bake and taste tests. How do we get that job?

(212) 727-1777
www.sevengramscaffe.com
Subway 4, 6 (28th St)

Sister locations Chelsea / Hudson Square

MON-FRI.	7:00am - 7:00pm
SAT-SUN.	8:00am - 7:00pm

First opened 2018
Roaster Seven Grams Caffé
Machine La Marzocco Strada EP, 3 groups
Grinder Nuova Simonelli Mythos One Clima Pro

Espresso	$3.00
Cappuccino	$4.50
Latte	$4.50

No. 124

Simon Sips

1185 Avenue of the Americas, Manhattan, NY 10036 | **Midtown West**

Simon Sips is in the business of making good coffee, plain and simple. It embraces a no-nonsense approach to providing exceptional coffee to those who are lucky enough to have found this unexpected shop, settled behind the lobby of a large office building. Head down to this industrious shop from the plaza entrance, open to the public from one of the side streets. The space has a simple, clean interior while their espressos are carefully pulled by attentive baristas. Simon Sips is a welcoming little resting place in the bustle of Midtown.

(212) 354-2100
www.simonsips.com
Subway 1, 2, 3 (42nd St) or 1 (50th St) or B, D, F, M (47th - 50th St - Rockefeller Center)

MON-FRI. 7:00am - 5:00pm
SAT-SUN. Closed

First opened 2012
Roaster Eldorado Coffee Roasters
Machine La Marzocco Linea, 2 groups
Grinder Mahlkönig EK 43

Espresso $3.00
Cappuccino $4.00
Latte $4.50

No. 125

St Kilda Coffee

328 West 44th Street, Manhattan, NY 10036 | **Hell's Kitchen**

The sunken entrance of this Melbourne inspired cafe brings a new meaning to the Down Under coffee experience. Easily missed but not easy to forget, St Kilda Coffee hosts a rotating line-up of high caliber roasters, offering seasonal single origin coffee for espresso, filter and cold brew with their expansive menu of 'stimulants'. Let the Kyoto on display tempt you, as this Japanese method of slow extraction patiently brews a deep earth-toned liquid, forcing you to sip a little slower, yet by the final gulp leaves you with the energy of a lightning bolt.

(646) 756-4660
www.stkildacoffee.com
Subway A, E (42nd St)

MON-FRI. 7:00am - 8:00pm
SAT-SUN. 8:00am - 8:00pm

First opened 2016
Roaster Sey Coffee Roasters, 49th Parallel Coffee Roasters, George Howell Coffee
Machine La Marzocco Strada EE, 3 groups
Grinder Mahlkönig Peak, Mahlkönig EK 43

Espresso $3.50
Cappuccino $4.75
Latte $4.75

No. 126

Stumptown Coffee Roasters Ace Hotel

Ace Hotel, 18 West 29th Street, Manhattan, NY 10001 | **Midtown West**

Stumptown has expanded considerably in the decade since opening their first New York outpost, but the consistency of the quality here hasn't changed a bit. They offer several types of cold brew including nitro. Grab a can to-go, and order a single origin Chemex pour over. Don't be fooled by the fact that these are not listed on the chalkboard menu; the baristas are verifiable wizards at extracting maximum flavor from the many single-origin bean offerings available.

(855) 711-3385
www.stumptowncoffee.com
Subway N, Q, R, W (28th St) or 4, 6 (28th St)

MON-FRI. 6:00am - 8:00pm
SAT-SUN. 7:00am - 8:00pm

First opened 2008
Roaster Stumptown Coffee Roasters
Machine La Marzocco Linea PB, 3 groups
Grinder Mazzer Luigi Robur E, Ditting

Espresso $3.25
Cappuccino $4.00
Latte $4.50

Sister locations Greenwich Village / Cobble Hill

No. 127

Taylor St Baristas

33 East 40th Street, Manhattan, NY 10016 | **Midtown East**

Aussie inspired Taylor St. Baristas is an extraordinary place to spend an afternoon. It's immediately welcoming and upstairs is an inspiring sight for midtowners: tons of space. Nothing here feels pretentious thanks to infectiously high-spirited baristas who gladly offer a free taste of each. They're as skilled as they are friendly. The espresso is excellent, as is their flat white made on the gleaming Victoria Arduino Black Eagle.

(212) 251-0719
www.taylor-st.com
Subway 4, 5, 6, 7, S (Grand Central)

MON-FRI. 7:00am - 6:00pm
SAT-SUN. Closed

First opened 2016
Roaster Taylor St Coffee
Machine Victoria Arduino Black Eagle, 3 groups x2
Grinder Nuova Simonelli Mythos x3, Mahlkönig EK 43

Espresso $3.50
Cappuccino $5.00
Latte $5.00

Think Coffee Gramercy

280 3rd Avenue, Manhattan, NY 10010 | **Gramercy**

This branch of Think just looks great. It has high ceilings and big windows on two sides of its L-shaped space, letting in lots of light and giving an airy feeling. The seating arrangement was designed with comfort in mind. Add a no-WiFi policy and you've got a formula for old-fashioned coffee conviviality in a very contemporary setting. Lots of people come for coffee to-go, but sitting down with a perfectly made macchiato or single-country pour over blend is by far the better option. Think Gramercy is a top choice in an area that provides plenty of it.

(212) 255-6452
www.thinkcoffee.com
Subway 6 (23rd St)

MON-FRI. 6:30am - 9:00pm
SAT-SUN. 7:00am - 9:00pm

First opened 2016
Roaster Think Coffee
Machine Synesso Cyncra, 3 groups
Grinder Mazzer Luigi Super Jolly

Espresso $3.25
Cappuccino $4.50
Latte $4.50

Sister locations Multiple locations

No. 129

Trademark Taste + Grind

38 West 36th Street, Manhattan, NY 10018 | **Midtown West**

Midtown Manhattan is full of all kinds of coffee-drinkers, and Trademark seems intent on subtly customizing the experience for each customer. If you're in a hurry and like vanilla lattes, they've got you covered. If you feel like staying a while, they'll make you an excellent, floral single-origin Phoenix pour over and serve it to you in a beautiful carafe. But you don't want to miss the espresso, extracted on a Mavam matte red espresso machine built into the bar - straight out of the production design of the movie 'Her', it's probably the most beautiful espresso machine you've ever seen. Plus there are only about 20 in the world.

(646) 858-2320
ingoodcompany.com
Subway B, D, F, M, N, Q, R, W (34th St - Herald Sq)

MON-FRI. 7:00am - 2:30pm
SAT-SUN. Closed

First opened 2016
Roaster Sweetleaf Coffee Roasters
Machine Mavam, 2 groups
Grinder Mazzer Luigi Kold, Mahlkönig EK 43

Espresso $3.50
Cappuccino $4.50
Latte $5.00

No. 130

Wattle Cafe

489 3rd Avenue, Manhattan, NY 10016 | **Kips Bay**

International in its scope, wonderfully casual, but blessed with boundless creativity and health-forward ingredients, Wattle represents so much of what is fascinating about the current coffee and food scene in Australia. Teaming up with exceptional Australian-owned roastery, Abbotsford Road, this relaxed cafe offers de rigueur Down Under drinks including the flat white as well as more nostalgic (milo milkshake) and exotic (charcoal turmeric latte) beverages. These are served alongside a single, diverse and delicious all-day brunch menu which keeps the space as invitingly informal as a coffee shop yet offers a range of experiences for patrons who can drop in whenever, linger for hours, or grab a bite to go.

(646) 918-7042
www.wattlecafe.com
Subway 4, 6 (33rd St)

MON-FRI.	7:00am - 6:00pm
SAT-SUN.	8:00am - 6:00pm

First opened 2017
Roaster Abbotsford Road Coffee Specialists
Machine La Marzocco Strada MP, 2 groups
Grinder Wega

Espresso	$3.25
Cappuccino	$4.25
Latte	$4.75

Sister locations Multiple locations

No. 131

Zibetto Espresso Bar

1385 6th Avenue, Manhattan, NY 10019 | **Midtown**

On a relatively uninspiring block of 6th Avenue, Zibetto's is a diamond in the rough. A very small, precious diamond. Somewhat more of a corridor, entering Zibetto Espresso Bar feels like walking into any small cafe in Italy. Espresso and all its derivatives are the order here, and luckily there's usually some time in line to decide which Italian pastries, paninis and decadent dolce to pair with coffee that packs a serious punch. Drinks are taken al banco (at the counter), behind which is the real joy of Zibettos, their sharply dressed baristas who provide a service which is vibrant, fast and, well, Italian!

(646) 707-0505
www.zibettoespresso.com
Subway F, N, Q, R, W (57th St)

Sister locations 6th Avenue / Park Avenue

MON-FRI.	7:00am - 7:00pm
SAT.	8:00am - 6:00pm
SUN.	8:00am - 5:00pm

First opened 2006
Roaster Zibetto
Machine Sanremo Opera, 3 groups
Grinder Sanremo

Espresso	$3.00
Cappuccino	$4.50
Latte	$5.00

No. 132

Photo: Ben Hider

From the Apollo Theatre in Harlem to the world-famous Metropolitan Museum of Art, upper northern Manhattan has a rich and varied cultural heritage. The Upper East Side boasts Museum Row, home to some of the greatest art and history museums in the country, as well as some of the best and most exclusive shopping in New York on Madison Avenue. The Upper West Side has a calmer feel, with the Lincoln Center for the performing Arts and The Museum of Natural History. In between sits the vast Central Park, New York's beloved urban oasis.

Upper Manhattan

Black Star Bakery

1597 York Avenue, Manhattan, NY 10028 | **Upper East Side**

Photo: Ben Hon

As you walk into this whitewashed Upper East Side cafe, expect your eyes to relax and nose to get very excited as it meets scents of fresh-baked cookies, croissants, and our favorite smell, coffee. Before you glaze over and walk straight to the counter housing their Faema Teorema and oven full of treats, check out the expanded breakfast and brunch menu with offerings from a light breakfast bowl to decadent Belgian waffles. The coffee here doesn't disappoint, with Oslo beans getting the expert treatment. Expect crowds young and old gathering in the crisp interior or out back in the grassy patio.

(646) 726-4546
www.blackstarbakery.com
Subway Q, R (86th St)

Sister locations Long Island City / Williamsburg

MON-FRI. 7:00am - 7:00pm
SAT-SUN. 8:00am - 7:00pm

First opened 2019
Roaster Oslo Coffee Roasters
Machine Faema Teorema, 3 groups
Grinder Mazzer Luigi

Espresso	$2.75
Cappuccino	$3.95
Latte	$3.95

No. 133

Bluestone Lane Upper East Side

1085 5th Avenue, Manhattan, NY 10128 | **Upper East Side**

Photo: Ben Hider

Aussie inspired Bluestone Lane has bagged a site that many cafes would kill for: a superb space in a Gothic-style church just across Fifth Avenue from Central Park. Sit in the sandstone interior or grab a table on the sidewalk. The food has a focus on virtue that doesn't sacrifice good flavour, while outstanding house-roasted beans get careful treatment on the La Marzocco. There's a notably warm welcome, and the barista skills extend to outstanding latte art: appropriate when the Guggenheim and the Met are a short walk away and Cooper Hewitt is right across the street.

(718) 374-6858
bluestonelane.com
Subway 4, 5, 6 (86th St)

Sister locations Multiple locations

MON-FRI. 7:30am - 7:00pm
SAT-SUN. 7:30am - 8:00pm

First opened 2015
Roaster Bluestone Lane
Machine La Marzocco Linea, 3 groups
Grinder Mazzer Luigi Robur E

Espresso $3.20
Cappuccino $4.25
Latte $4.25

No. 134

Box Kite NYC

128 West 72nd Street, Manhattan, NY 10023 | **Upper West Side**

The lower end of the Upper West Side does not exactly overflow with places for a superior cup, which makes it all the more thrilling that Box Kite chose to open a branch here in 2015. The place is small, with seating for just six people, so the emphasis is inevitably on coffee to take away rather than drink on the premises. But it's an attractive place to sit, and being a WiFi-free zone, it's something of a refuge from the busy world outside.

Subway 1, 2, 3 (72nd St)

MON-FRI. 7:00am - 6:00pm
SAT-SUN. 8:00am - 6:00pm

First opened 2015
Roaster Multiple roasters
Machine Synesso MVP Hydra, 2 groups
Grinder Mahlkönig Peak, Mahlkönig EKK43

Espresso	Varies
Cappuccino	$4.50
Latte	$5.10

No. 135

Café Jax

318 East 84th Street, Manhattan, NY 10028 | **Upper East Side**

Café Jax is a dream of a neighborhood coffee spot. It's a place where all drinks are taken seriously - even as the sense of childhood is preserved in pours such as cold brew ice cream float and lavender lemonade. Dallis Bros. beans make up the house blend, enjoyable in numerous hot and cold forms as you eat a salad, sandwich or baked good. The long front room is lovely but the large downstairs seating space, and especially the garden, are to be admired.

(212) 510-7084
www.cafejaxnyc.com
Subway Q (86th St)

MON-FRI. 7:00am - 8:00pm
SAT-SUN. 8:00am - 8:00pm

First opened 2014
Roaster Dallis Bros. Coffee
Machine La Marzocco Linea, 2 groups
Grinder Mazzer Luigi Major E

Espresso	$3.00
Cappuccino	$4.00 / $5.50
Latte	$4.25 / $4.75

No. 136

The Chipped Cup

3610 Broadway, Manhattan, NY 10031 | **Harlem**

This Harlem anchor offers great coffee in a comforting environment. It boasts fresh pastries from Balthazar and toasted bagel sandwiches, if you're really peckish, to go along with well-drawn shots of Counter Culture espresso. The space is fitted out with lots of tables for all the computer-clacking workers, and there's also a sweet backyard if you're feeling like a breath of fresh air instead.

(212) 368-8881
www.chippedcupcoffee.com
Subway 1 (145th St)

MON-FRI. 7:00am - 8:00pm
SAT-SUN. 8:00am - 8:00pm

First opened 2012
Roaster Counter Culture Coffee
Machine La Marzocco GB5, 2 groups
Grinder Mazzer Luigi Robur E

Espresso	$3.25
Cappuccino	$4.25
Latte	$4.75

Dear Mama

308 East 109th Street, Manhattan, NY 10029 | **Harlem**

Photo: Casandra Rosario

Dear Mama was the first specialty coffee venue to open in this area of East Harlem, and being the first in a neighborhood still relatively un-gentrified by Manhattan standards would have to be regarded as bold verging on risky. But the bold move turned out to be a shrewd one: they started out strong and have only become 'busier and busier.' Dear Mama set out to be a 'neighborhood hub,' and there's definitely a great local feel here, right down to the pictures by local artists hanging on the walls.

(929) 279-2225
www.dearmamacoffee.com
Subway 4, 6 (110th St) or 1, 2 (125th St)

Sister locations West Harlem

MON-SUN. 7:00am - 7:00pm

First opened 2016
Roaster Dear Mama and guests
Machine Synesso MVP Hydra, 2 groups
Grinder Mahlkönig Peak, Nuova Simonelli Mythos One Clima Pro

Espresso	$3.50
Cappuccino	$4.50
Latte	$5.00

No. 138

Double Dutch Espresso City College

1616 Amsterdam Avenue, Manhattan, NY 10031 | **Harlem**

With the huge CCNY campus just outside, Double Dutch Espresso could probably do good business even if it sold diner coffee. But this tiny, chilled Hamilton Heights venue shows a deep commitment to getting high quality from its Counter Culture beans - and it's a very nice place to sit, as well. All espresso-based drinks are available on ice if you don't like it hot, and the simple food offering majors on bagels and highly tempting baked goods. In an area that isn't rich in specialty coffee, Double Dutch is a real find.

(917) 475-1120
www.doubledutchespresso.com
Subway 1 (137th St - City College)

MON-FRI.	7:00am - 7:00pm
SAT-SUN.	8:00am - 5:00pm

First opened 2016
Roaster Counter Culture Coffee
Machine La Marzocco GB5, 2 groups
Grinder Mazzer Luigi Robur E

Espresso	$3.25
Cappuccino	$4.25
Latte	$4.75

Sister locations South Harlem / South Bronx

No. 139

Double Dutch Espresso South Harlem

2194 Frederick Douglass Boulevard, Manhattan, NY 10026 | **Harlem**

This busy Harlem shop offers a delightful atmosphere for an afternoon coffee respite. Double Dutch serves locally baked treats, fresh home-made sandwiches and great coffee to charge you through the last few pages of that book you're just aching to finish. There is plenty of seating in a winsome atmosphere, with antique accents that make it feel warm and inviting. They keep two espressos on bar at a time, a blend and a rotating single origin, so be sure to ask for what's available.

(646) 429-8834
www.doubledutchespresso.com
Subway B, C (116th St)

MON-FRI.	7:00am - 8:00pm
SAT-SUN.	8:00am - 8:00pm

First opened 2014
Roaster Counter Culture Coffee
Machine La Marzocco GB5
Grinder Mazzer Luigi E

Espresso	$3.25
Cappuccino	$4.00
Latte	$4.75

Sister locations South Bronx / City College

No. 140

Gregorys Coffee Upper East Side

878 Lexington Avenue, Manhattan, NY 10065 | **Upper East Side**

Gregorys must be doing something right. At the time of writing it has 23 NYC branches and all do a steady-to-roaring trade. This one has an enviable location, with Hunter College nearby, and while the college supplied most business in the early days, now it's much more broadly based. WiFi all week is one draw, but the big room (especially in the back), relaxed vibe, and great brewing from the well-trained team is surely more important. Milky drinks are excellent, and so are single-origin coffees from the drip brewers.

(917) 388-3850
www.gregoryscoffee.com
Subway F, Q (Lexington Ave - 63rd St)

Sister locations Multiple locations

MON-THU.	6:00am - 7:30pm
FRI.	6:00am - 7:00pm
SAT.	7:00am - 7:00pm
SUN.	7:00am - 6:00pm

First opened 2015
Roaster Gregorys Coffee
Machine La Marzocco Linea PB, 3 groups
Grinder Mazzer Luigi Kold

Espresso	$3.00
Cappuccino	$4.00
Latte	$4.65

No. 141

Hutch + Waldo

247 East 81st Street, Manhattan, NY 10028 | **Upper East Side**

Rolling up the front door of this garage-turned-cafe and finding a fresh interior of beech wood and abundant plant life, Hutch + Waldo will have you feeling as if you've stumbled upon a beach-side hangout. The park-adjacent location makes it the perfect spot to grab a 'brekkie sando' and silky flat white to take-away. Far from all style no substance, Hutch + Waldo champions fair trade, small batch coffee. The result is a citrusy bright cold brew, expertly handled coffee and signature lattes including almond-turmeric and macadamia-beet, supplied to a constant stream of Upper East Side caffeine addicts and health nuts alike.

(646) 266-3648
www.hutchandwaldo.cafe
Subway Q, R (86th St)

MON-SUN. 7:00am - 5:00pm

First opened 2017
Roaster Hutch + Waldo Roasters
Machine La Marzocco Strada AV, 3 groups
Grinder Mahlkönig EK 43, Mazzer Luigi Robur E x2

Espresso	$3.25
Cappuccino	$4.00
Latte	$4.00

No. 142

Irving Farm New York Upper East Side

1424 3rd Avenue, Manhattan, NY 10028 | **Upper East Side**

Coffee connoisseurs cannot miss Irving Farm's grand Upper East Side location. This 1,700 square foot space boasts Irving Farm's largest, both in terms of the seating area and the kitchen. It is a space that affords customers the luxury of choice: either sit in the front bar and absorb the bustling energy, or relax in the mezzanine area, where there is plenty of seating spread throughout. A delicious array of donuts from Underwest Donuts is the perfect accompaniment to any Irving Farm coffee. As always, Irving Farm is all about delivering a quality brew, and this location features espresso, filter, and by-the-cup Kalita pour overs. What's not to like about this beautiful venue?

(212) 206-0707
irvingfarm.com
Subway 4, 5 (86th St) or 6 (77th St)

MON-FRI. 7:00am - 7:00pm
SAT-SUN. 8:00am - 8:00pm

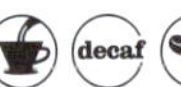

First opened 2016
Roaster Irving Farm New York
Machine La Marzocco Linea PB, 2 groups
Grinder Nuova Simonelli Mythos One Clima Pro

Espresso $3.25
Cappuccino $4.50
Latte $4.75

Sister locations Multiple locations

No. 143

Joe Coffee Company Upper East Side

1045 Lexington Avenue, Manhattan, NY 10021 | **Upper East Side**

Joe has seen new competition arrive since it landed on the Upper East Side in 2011, but it remains a hot favorite with locals. The look is more downtown than uptown, with bare brick and some out-there lampshades. And you'll be lucky to find a seat: there are just a few, in the window and at a communal table. All the hallmark Joe qualities are here in the cup, from great beans (blends or single-origin) through to expert brewing and dazzling latte art.

(212) 988-2500
joecoffeecompany.com
Subway 4, 5, 6 (77th St)

Sister locations Multiple locations

MON-SUN. 7:00am - 8:00pm

First opened 2011
Roaster Joe Coffee Company
Machine La Marzocco GB5, 2 groups
Grinder Nuova Simonelli Mythos

Espresso	$3.03
Cappuccino	$4.04
Latte	$4.04

Kuro Kuma Espresso & Coffee

121 La Salle Street, Manhattan, NY 10027 | **Harlem**

Part of Kuro Kuma's success arises from location: this part of Morningside Heights isn't packed with good coffee purveyors. But Kuro Kuma would be smashing it anywhere, however stiff the competition, because this tiny place (seating for six or so) is sensationally good. The coffee is made from Counter Culture beans by highly skilled baristas who take equal care with every type of drink. Even iced coffee, so often a pallid potion, turns to magic here. No wonder Columbia students (and just about everyone else) line up to buy.

(347) 577-3177
Subway 1 (125th St)

MON-SAT. 7:00am - 7:30pm
SUN. 8:00am - 7:30pm

First opened 2012
Roaster Counter Culture Coffee
Machine La Marzocco GB5, 2 groups
Grinder Mazzer Luigi SRL

Espresso $3.00
Cappuccino $4.00
Latte $4.00

No. 145

Le Reveil Coffee

1322 2nd Avenue, Manhattan, NY 10021 | **Upper East Side**

Le Reveil is the type of cafe you go to for a long lunch with a friend. The food is simple, fresh and delicious, while the service is unfalteringly friendly and helpful. Even during peak times, you can always expect to find a seat and a smile at this new Upper East Side establishment. While the location may be compact, you can expect a full-bodied cup of joe here, tasty and brimming with flavor. Their robust Turkish coffee is not to be missed either. There's also a variety of tasty toasts, salads, sandwiches and baked goods on offer with an authentic Mediterranean twist.

(347) 216-9453
www.lereveilcoffee.com
Subway Q, R (72nd St)

MON-SUN. 6:00am - 8:00pm

First opened 2018
Roaster Intelligentsia Coffee
Machine La Marzocco Linea PB, 2 groups
Grinder Mazzer Luigi x2

Espresso $3.25
Cappuccino $4.00
Latte $4.50

No. 146

Lenox Coffee

60 West 129th Street, Manhattan, NY 10027 | **Harlem**

Since sisters Rosa and Monika took over in 2016 this unassuming neighborhood spot in Central Harlem has transformed into a specialty coffee house and micro-roastery. Lenox Coffee draws on Harlem's rich cultural history and vibrant art scene. Low ceilings and dimmed lights provide an intimate space for creatives to enjoy seasonal, single-origin drip and perfectly balanced espresso blends served alongside pastries and house-made brunch items. Most Mondays they open until late, so skip the Harlem Jazz museum next door and settle in for a brilliant open mic night.

(646) 833-7839
www.lenoxcoffee.com
Subway 2, 3, 4, 5, 6 (125th St)

MON.	7:00am - 8:00pm
TUE-FRI.	7:00am - 7:00pm
SAT-SUN.	8:00am - 7:00pm

First opened 2011
Roaster Lenox Coffee
Machine La Marzocco Linea EE, 2 groups
Grinder Mazzer Luigi

Espresso	$2.75
Cappuccino	$3.75
Latte	$4.00

Manhattanville Coffee

142 Edgecombe Avenue, Manhattan, NY 10030 | **Harlem**

Originally from performance backgrounds, married owners Michael and German are rising to the role of big city coffee shop owners with the small-town warmth and generosity to match the 'ville' of their namesake. Manhattanville feels intimate and familiar, or maybe that's because it is becoming one of New York movie directors' favorite locations for shoots! The design is generous in style and substance with a diverse seating design of couches, bar counters and communal tables to foster collaboration, private study and socializing all in one cohesive space. Parlor coffee on order, roasted locally, is sweet, bright and citrusy with a rotation of seasonal specials composed while you watch the seasons change out the window.

(646) 781-9900
www.manhattanvillecoffee.com
Subway A, B, C, D (145th St)

MON-FRI. 7:00am - 7:00pm
SAT-SUN. 8:00am - 7:00pm

First opened 2014
Roaster Parlor Coffee
Machine La Marzocco GB5 EE, 2 groups
Grinder Mahlkönig EK 43

Espresso $2.75
Cappuccino $3.75
Latte $4.25

Sister locations Lucille's

No. 148

The Monkey Cup

1730 Amsterdam Avenue, Manhattan, NY 10031 | **Upper Manhattan**

Laura Leonardi, the Argentinian-born owner of Monkey Cup, trained as a dentist but has now drilled deep into the essence of coffee culture. Her diminutive drop is one of the best places in Harlem for superior cups, either espresso-based or brewed - including the slow-drip cold-brew Kyoto method. The espresso beans change every three months ('We like the variables') and pour overs are single-origin. This is a warm, friendly place where people love to talk to each other. If you want to guarantee a smile on your face, order a 'Monkeyccino.'

(646) 664-7483
themonkeycup.com
Subway A, B, C, D (145th St)

MON-SUN. 7:00am - 7:00pm

First opened 2015
Roaster Irving Farm New York
Machine La Marzocco Linea, 3 groups
Grinder Mahlkönig K30

Espresso	$2.85
Cappuccino	$3.40
Latte	$3.70

Sister locations Harlem

No. 149

Moss Café

3260 Johnson Avenue, Bronx, NY 10463 | **Kingsbridge**

They're all about things local and fresh at Moss Café, as the shop bustles with neighbors and families who come in to enjoy the healthy food and charming environment. One of the first Third Wave coffee shops to come to the Bronx, Moss Café shares Stumptown beans with the neighbors, alongside house made baked goods and a seasonal menu that all happens to be Kosher too. You'll even find gluten free and dairy-free items, so it's pretty easy to find something delicious and wholesome to go along with your lovely latte.

(347) 275-5000
www.mosscafeny.com
Subway 1 (231st St)

MON-THU.	7:00am - 9:00pm
FRI.	7:00am - 4:00pm
SAT.	Closed
SUN.	8:00am - 8:00pm

First opened 2015
Roaster Stumptown Coffee Roasters,
Machine La Marzocco GB5 EE, 2 groups
Grinder Mazzer Luigi Kony E

Espresso	$3.00
Cappuccino	$4.25
Latte	$4.75

No. 150

Oslo Coffee Roasters Upper East Side

422 East 75th Street, Manhattan, NY 10021 | **Upper East Side**

Oslo's Yorkville location is a tiny neighborhood caffeinery with a big heart. The baristas welcome local customers as if they were old friends - which many of them appear to be. The real star here is the old, lovingly maintained authentic San Marco espresso machine - a manual job complete with gleaming levers. Baristas pull great shots of Oslo's creamy espresso blend using those levers, and watching them at work is an all-too-rare pleasure.

(718) 782-0332
oslocoffee.com
Subway Q (72nd St) or 6 (77th St)

Sister locations Williamsburg (Bedford Ave) / Williamsburg (Roebling St)

MON-FRI.	7:00am - 7:00pm
SAT-SUN.	8:00am - 7:00pm (6:00pm in winter)

First opened 2011
Roaster Oslo Coffee Roasters
Machine San Marco Leva, 3 groups
Grinder Mazzer Luigi Major, Ditting

Espresso	$3.25
Cappuccino	$4.25
Latte	$4.25

No. 151

PlantShed Cafe

555 Columbus Avenue, Manhattan, NY 10024 | **Upper West Side**

PlantShed Cafe is the most recent coffee spot to set down its roots in the Upper West Side, fusing fresh blooms and exquisite coffee in one very green space. Working with Brooklyn-based roaster Partners Coffee to craft floral-inspired blends, this sensory paradise features an extensive coffee menu of bright, nuanced brews. They further express their love of plants through a seasonal selection of iced lattes garnished with edible flowers and a formidable selection of six plant-based milk alternatives. Escape the concrete and recharge in this beautiful indoor jungle.

(212) 662-4400
www.plantshed.com
Subway 1, 2 (86th St)

MON-SAT. 7:00am - 8:00pm
SUN. 7:00am - 7:00pm

First opened 2018
Roaster Partners Coffee
Machine La Marzocco Linea PB, 2 groups
Grinder Nuova Simonelli Mythos Plus, Mazzer Luigi Robur S

Espresso $3.50
Cappuccino $4.50
Latte $4.75

Plowshares Coffee Bloomingdale

2730 Broadway, Manhattan, NY 10025 | **Upper West Side**

Plowshares opened this spot quietly, but word of mouth travels quickly in this town, and their wonderfully prepared coffees are making waves among the caffeinated elite. They roast their own coffees and serve them with care at this 11-seat shop. They only have one blend here, while all the others are single origin varieties from across the coffee-producing world. They offer at least two batch-brewed coffees at a time, a pour over bar, and both a regular and nitrogen-infused cold brew that's extra rich and caffeinated.

(212) 222-0280
www.plowsharescoffee.com
Subway 1 (103rd St)

MON-FRI. 7:00am - 8:00pm
SAT-SUN. 8:00am - 7:00pm

First opened 2014
Roaster Plowshares Coffee Roasters
Machine Slayer V3, 2 groups
Grinder Mahlkönig K30 Twin, Mahlkönig EK 43

Espresso	$3.25
Cappuccino	$4.50
Latte	$5.00

No. 153

PROOF Coffee Roasters (ACP)

2286 7th Avenue, Manhattan, NY 10030 | **Harlem**

Impeccably welcoming, the young and enthusiastic team at PROOF are eager to guide you through the diverse coffee menu, which features coffee options harder to come by in the surrounding neighborhood. Sitting inside, light streams from the back and front windows of the cafe providing the perfect light to frame work by local artists, and for the artistry of preparation for V60 and Chemex coffees. The slow-form caffeinated permutations, combined with a playlist of old jazz, MacBooks and modern art creates an atmosphere that is at once nostalgic and ultramodern, a reflection of New York City itself.

(212) 234-8290
www.proof.coffee
Subway 2, 3, A, B, C, D (135th St)

MON-FRI. 7:00am - 6:00pm
SAT-SUN. 8:00am - 6:00pm

First opened 2018
Roaster PROOF Coffee Roasters
Machine La Marzocco Linea AV, 2 groups
Grinder Mahlkönig K30 Vario Air

Espresso $3.00
Cappuccino $4.00
Latte $4.50

Sister locations SVK / Carmel Place / Nassau / 5th Avenue

No. 154

Ralph's Coffee

888 Madison Avenue, Manhattan, NY 10021 | **Upper East Side**

Launched as the set for a Ralph Lauren fashion show, Ralph's decadent cafe lounge housed inside the brand's Madison Avenue flagship location is now fully operational, offering visitors a unique and experiential expression of the timeless fashion brand. Entering feels like springtime in the Hamptons, welcoming and indulgent, with a fit-out of forest green leather booths, signature Tea House Floral wallpaper, chandeliers, and marble tables, paying homage to the brand's all-American heritage. In addition to beautiful baked goods from Mah-Ze-Dahr Bakery, Ralph's merchandise, mugs, shirts and coffee beans are for sale, but this is no gimmick. Teaming up with La Colombe to create special blends, including a Swiss Water Process decaf for the caffeine-averse, the espresso preparation is impressive: as fine and floral as the entire RL experience.

No. 155

MON-SAT. 8:00am - 7:00pm
SUN. 9:00am - 6:00pm

First opened 2018
Roaster La Colombe Coffee Roasters
Machine La Marzocco FB80, 2 groups
Grinder Bunn

Espresso $3.50
Cappuccino $5.50
Latte $5.00

(212) 434-8000
www.ralphlauren.com/ralphs-coffee-feat
Subway 1, 2 (Franklin St)

Sister locations Rockefeller Center / Flatiron District

Photos: Carl Timpone

Shuteye Coffee

137 West 116th Street, Manhattan, NY 10026 | **Harlem**

Shuteye takes its name from a mountain peak in Yosemite, where owners Guy and Joe grew up playing music and hiking, and provides a petite and peaceful sanctuary which speaks to their early years. The front window overflows with plant life, while jazz encompasses the space and dulls noise from the bustling Harlem streets. You'll almost always find one of the boys behind the Strada EP, providing a spirited explanation of the unique and exciting variety of beans on offer for your espresso, thanks to a close collaboration with East One Coffee Roasters. If you're not sure what to order, start with a perfectly pulled espresso and they'll help you build your perfect brew from there.

Sitting in the space with a cortado prepared with funky and fruity natural Colombian beans, and watching smiling faces order 'the usual', it's clear how connected Shuteye is to their community; it's more than just coffee bringing people back.

No. 156

MON-SUN. 7:00am - 5:00pm

First opened 2017
Roaster East One Coffee Roasters
Machine La Marzocco Strada EP, 2 groups
Grinder Mahlkönig EK 43, Mahlkönig K30

Espresso $3.00
Cappuccino $3.75
Latte $4.00

(646) 596-9622
www.shuteyecoffee.com
Subway 2, 3 (116th St)

Variety Coffee Roasters Upper East Side

1269 Lexington Avenue, Manhattan, NY 10028 | **Upper East Side**

The first thing that strikes you as you walk into Variety's UES location is the old-school beauty of this space, with custom woodwork everywhere, from the walls to the exquisite La Marzocco Linea espresso machine on the bar. With a growing, authentic brand that now stretches from Bushwick to Uptown Manhattan, Variety is on the up and up, bringing their straightforward menu and Lucky Shot Espresso to more and more (and increasingly discerning) neighborhoods across the city. The cold brew is a perfect refreshment on a warm day, but you can never go wrong with one of their beautifully fragrant espresso-based drinks. Variety allows visitors to enjoy their experience and focus on what really matters: great coffee in a stunning, but unpretentious environment.

(212) 289-2104
varietycoffeeroasters.com
Subway 4, 5, 6 (86th St - Lexington Ave)

MON-SUN. 7:00am - 9:00pm

First opened 2017
Roaster Variety Coffee Roasters
Machine La Marzocco Linea AV, 3 groups
Grinder Mahlkönig Peak

Espresso $3.00
Cappuccino $4.00
Latte $4.50

Sister locations Bushwick / Chelsea / Greenpoint / Williamsburg

No. 157

Photo: Tyler Nix

The largely residential neighborhoods of Park Slope, Kensington, Ditmas Park, Crown Heights and Prospect Gardens make up this area of Brooklyn. Kensington and Ditmas Park still retain many examples of beautiful Victorian architecture, while Prospect Heights is known for its rich cultural history. The Brooklyn Botanical Gardens, The Brooklyn Museum and The Pratt Institute all be found there. Park Slope itself, with its picturesque tree-lined streets, historic brownstones, popular restaurants and shops, is a great neighborhood to explore.

Park Slope & Surrounding

Blue Bottle Coffee Park Slope

203 7th Avenue, Brooklyn, NY 11215 | **Park Slope**

Situated in a more residential area of the neighborhood, just a short walk from Prospect Park, Blue Bottle Park Slope is exceptionally accommodating to its patrons - offering stroller parking outside, highchairs inside, and a wonderful array of trendy wooden toys for their youngest clientele. Of course, there is beautiful seating for adults too, not to mention fantastic brews. With its bright, airy layout and quiet environment, it's the sort of place one can turn to for refuge, inspiration, or both. You can also learn the art of creating a perfect brew yourself at their weekly coffee making classes. With relaxing off-sidewalk outdoor seating and no WiFi, it is the perfect spot to kick back in the sun and socialize with friends.

(510) 653-3394
bluebottlecoffee.com
Subway F, G (7th Ave)

MON-FRI. 7:00am - 6:00pm
SAT-SUN. 7:30am - 6:30pm

First opened 2016
Roaster Blue Bottle Coffee
Machine Kees van der Westen Spirit, 2 groups
Grinder Baratza

Espresso $3.50
Cappuccino $4.50
Latte $5.00

Sister locations Multiple locations

No. 158

Brunswick

240 Prospect Park West, Brooklyn, NY 11215 | **Park Slope**

Don't be fooled by the unassuming entrance to Brunswick. Once you delve deeper, through the idyllic white, cacti-filled passageway, you'll discover a 40-seat enclosed garden. Whether nestling up in modern booth seating or joining a communal table, you'll be surrounded by 360 degrees of plant life and sunlight. The coffee on offer features well-executed espresso drinks served with a noteworthy all-day brunch menu combining classic Southern and Australian brunch items. Brunswick uses Battenkill Valley grass-fed milk, adding a sweetness and creamy mouthfeel to their coffee, leaving the flavor of Counter Culture's impeccable beans lingering on the tongue.

(718) 788-1237
www.brunswickcafe.com
Subway F, G (15 St - Prospect Park)

MON-FRI. 8:00am - 4:00pm
SAT-SUN. 8:30am - 4:00pm

First opened 2014
Roaster Counter Culture Coffee
Machine La Marzocco Linea, 2 groups
Grinder Mazzer Luigi SRL

Espresso $3.25
Cappuccino $4.00
Latte $4.50

Sister locations Milk Bar (Prospect Heights) / Milk Bar (Park Slope)

No. 159

Café Regular du Nord

158a Berkeley Place, Brooklyn, NY 11217 | **Park Slope**

Good things come in small packages. Café Regular du Nord is a beautiful cafe with vintage vibes, from the funky painting on the wall to the crystal chandelier. The espresso-based beverages are great, but the best quality of this cafe is its versatile menu, where there is something for adults and kids alike. Not a coffee drinker, or bringing the kids with you? No need to worry, delicious Jacques Torres hot chocolate is served here. Teachers and students, be sure to take advantage of the discounts offered.

(718) 783-0673
www.caferegular.com
Subway B, Q (7th Ave) or R (Union St)

Sister locations Park Slope

MON-SUN. 7:00am - 7:00pm

First opened 2009
Roaster La Colombe Coffee Roasters
Machine La Marzocco GB5 EE, 2 groups
Grinder Mazzer Luigi Super Jolly E

Espresso	$2.25
Cappuccino	$4.00
Latte	$4.00

No. 160

Clever Blend

97 5th Avenue, Brooklyn, NY 11217 | **Park Slope**

Clever Blend truly lives up to its name - it is a haven for coffee enthusiasts who are also lovers of literature. With a counter that doubles as a bookshelf, there is never a shortage of literary works to indulge in while sipping your delicious cold brew. The staff are friendly, and the rotating menu of single-origin coffee never disappoints. Featuring plenty of seating and great music, Clever Blend is the perfect spot to meet with friends in the latest hip, intellectual environment nestled in Park Slope.

(718) 782-7470
www.cleverblend.com
Subway 2, 3, 4 (Bergen St)

MON-FRI.	6:30am - 6:30pm
SAT.	7:00am - 7:00pm
SUN.	7:30am - 6:30pm

First opened 2017
Roaster Clever Blend
Machine Elektra Barlume, 2 groups
Grinder Mahlkönig EK 43, Mazzer Luigi

Espresso	$3.00
Cappuccino	$4.50
Latte	$4.50

Sister locations Long Island City / Williamsburg (coming soon)

No. 161

Coffee Mob

1514 Newkirk Avenue, Brooklyn, NY 11226 | **Ditmas Park**

If you're looking for quality (both of the roast and musical variety) look no further than Coffee Mob. Situated in a lovely corner spot in the Flatbush neighborhood, this venue promises expertly brewed, single-origin espresso. The beans are roasted in house on a rotating basis, sourced from fair-trade plantations around the world. In addition to its roast, the venue offers a variety of sandwiches and pastries, making it the perfect lunch spot. Vinyl turntables sit next to the La Marzocco GB5, allowing the baristas to double as DJs and offer some sweet tunes.

(917) 545-5857
coffeemob.com
Subway B, Q (Newkirk Plaza)

MON-FRI.	7:00am - 6:30pm
SAT-SUN.	8:00am - 6:30pm

First opened 2013
Roaster Coffee Mob
Machine La Marzocco GB5 MP, 2 groups
Grinder Mahlkönig Peak

Espresso	$3.50
Cappuccino	$3.75
Latte	$4.25

Sister locations Coney Island

No. 162

Everyman Espresso Park Slope

162 5th Avenue, Brooklyn, NY 11217 | **Park Slope**

Situated in quaint Park Slope, the 'Damn Fine Coffee', as proclaimed in neon lettering, is a satisfying addition to Brooklyn's bustling coffee scene, because it is damn fine coffee. Counter Culture beans are brewed to perfection on the La Marzocco, and the matcha latte might just be the best in the borough. In addition to the brew, the shop itself is a visual delight with its colorful tiled walls and well-designed lighting. People come in with family, friends, and their devices - a nice mix that creates a genuinely friendly neighborhood cafe.

www.everymanespresso.com
Subway D, N, R, W (Union St)

MON-FRI. 7:00am - 6:00pm
SAT-SUN. 8:00am - 6:00pm

First opened 2017
Roaster Counter Culture Coffee
Machine La Marzocco Strada, 2 groups
Grinder Nuova Simonelli Mythos One x2

Espresso $3.75
Cappuccino $4.75
Latte $5.25

Sister locations Soho / East Village

No. 163

Gorilla Coffee

472 Bergen Street, Brooklyn, NY 11217 | **Park Slope**

Photo: Jael Marschner

Gorilla Coffee, is a big, modern, functionally decorated place with very fifties-looking tables. Somehow none of that makes it feel institutional, because this is a comfortable place to sit and hang out. Gorilla has been roasting in Brooklyn since 2002 and their full variety is shown best in the Chemex or pour over, but espresso-based drinks are made to the same high standards. Baked goods are very popular, but don't be surprised if the selection's shrunk if you get there later in the day.

(347) 987-3766
www.gorillacoffee.com
Subway 2, 3 (Bergen St)

MON-SAT.	7:00am - 8:00pm
SAT.	8:00am - 9:00pm
SUN.	8:00am - 8:00pm

First opened 2014
Roaster Gorilla Coffee
Machine La Marzocco Strada, 3 groups
Grinder Mazzer Luigi Robur

Espresso	$3.00
Cappuccino	$4.00
Latte	$4.50

No. 164

Hungry Ghost

253 Flatbush Avenue, Brooklyn, NY 11217 | **Prospect Heights**

Sleek is the first word that comes to mind upon entering Hungry Ghost. With its cool gray undertones and comfortable seating, it is the perfect spot to relax with a cold brew and one of their much sought after scones. Conversation and community is encouraged within the space, as laptop use is restricted to a select area. This emphasis on community, combined with the quality products, makes Hungry Ghost a Prospect Heights destination for everyone from coffee connoisseurs to creative collaborators.

(718) 483-8666
www.hungryghostcoffee.com
Subway 2, 3, 4 (Bergen St) or (Atlantic Ave - Barclays Ctr)

MON-SUN. 6:00am - 8:00pm

First opened 2012
Roaster Stumptown Coffee Roasters
Machine La Marzocco GB5, 2 groups
Grinder Mazzer Luigi

Espresso	$3.50
Cappuccino	$4.50
Latte	$4.75

Sister locations Multiple locations

No. 165

Kos Kaffe

251 5th Avenue, Brooklyn, NY 11215 | **Park Slope**

For the patrons of New York's increasing proliferation of hyper-modern, minimalist cafe's, Kos Kaffe may feel like unadulterated chaos. But we think the mismatched tables and chairs, chandeliers and handwritten signs all add to its charm, creating the effect of entering a modest and eclectic country home. Husband and wife team, a long-time coffee roaster and a chef, have created a generous space for the community focused on communion, quality, and craftsmanship. The gentle smells of house-made breakfast and lunch from the grill and of toasty coffee beans from their drum roaster will have you feeling right at home.

(718) 768-6868
www.koskaffe.com
Subway 2, 3, 4 (Bergen St) or G, F (4th Ave - 9th St)

MON-FRI.	7:00am - 7:00pm
SAT-SUN.	8:00am - 7:00pm

First opened 2012
Roaster Kos Kaffe
Machine Faema, 2 groups
Grinder Mazzer Luigi Major E

Espresso	$3.00
Cappuccino	$4.00
Latte	$4.00

No. 166

Little Zelda

728 Franklin Avenue, Brooklyn, NY 11238 | **Crown Heights**

Little Zelda is the quintessential neighborhood spot, a charming little space where coffee isn't just a beverage but something that brings people together. You'll find local writers and readers getting literary while sipping lattes at this delightfully vintage cafe with well-used and ever lovely Partners coffees. There's a community board where people looking for roommates or apartments may post to find a match. This cozy shop and its cheery staff make Little Zelda a lovely little home away from home.

(802) 491-7711
Subway S (Park Pl) or 2, 3, 4, 5, A, C (Franklin Ave)

MON-SUN. 7:00am - 5:00pm

First opened 2012
Roaster Partners Coffee
Machine La Marzocco Linea, 2 groups
Grinder Bunn

Espresso	$2.50
Cappuccino	$3.00
Latte	$3.50

No. 167

Milk and Honey Café

1119 Newkirk Avenue, Brooklyn, NY 11230 | **Ditmas Park**

Trendy, hip, and delicious - these are just a few words to describe Milk and Honey, a bustling cafe on Newkirk Avenue. Upon entering this unique cafe, there is a lush plant wall that creates a striking first impression. Order at the counter and then find a place to sit, we recommend choosing a spot on the outdoor patio if weather permits. More cafe than coffee shop, the food is truly superb and their coffee never disappoints either. Try the Crème Brulee French Toast at brunch; a local favorite.

(718) 513-0441
www.milkandhoneycafeny.com
Subway B, Q (Newkirk Plaza)

MON-SUN. 7:00am - 8:00pm

First opened 2013
Roaster Counter Culture Coffee
Machine La Marzocco Strada AV, 3 groups
Grinder Nuova Simonelli Mythos

Espresso $2.75
Cappuccino $3.50
Latte $4.00

Sister locations Optimistic Cafe

No. 168

Milk Bar

620 Vanderbilt Avenue, Brooklyn, NY 11238 | **Prospect Heights**

Tiny, light-filled Milk Bar is run like a restaurant - a waiter acts as host, seating your party when you arrive. In other hands, this type of set-up could feel highly-strung, but the staff are so pleasant that having the attention of a waiter is a relaxed affair. Located in Prospect Heights, it's a quiet neighborhood shop, but is also good enough to go out of your way for. You can't go wrong with the drinks here - Counter Culture provides the beans - but honor the shop's Australian roots and go with the excellent, strong flat white.

(718) 230-0844
www.milkbarbrooklyn.com
Subway B, Q (7th Ave)

Sister locations Park Slope

MON-FRI. 7:30am - 4:00pm
SAT-SUN. 8:00am - 4:00pm

First opened 2009
Roaster Counter Culture Coffee
Machine La Marzocco Linea, 2 groups
Grinder Mazzer Luigi

Espresso	$3.50
Cappuccino	$4.00
Latte	$4.50

No. 169

Orso Coffee

1745 Sheepshead Bay Road, Brooklyn, NY 11235 | **Sheepshead Bay**

Orso perfectly nails the style, vibe, and flavor profile of what you imagine a bay-side coffee shop to be. The 600-square-foot shop is flooded with natural light, shining upon exposed copper piping and a neon mural by local artist Raisa Nosova. While offering specialty brews to delight coffee zealots, the medium-roast beans by Queens-based For Five, communal bar seating and diverse customer base keep the space grounded. On offer is a selection of quality pastries and sandwiches, along with a curated selection of health-focused small bites to go. They even have cold brew and kombucha on tap, and everything tastes better on tap, right?

(718) 484-9250
www.orsocoffee.com
Subway B, Q (Sheepshead Bay)

MON-FRI.	7:00am - 7:00pm
SAT.	8:00am - 7:00pm
SUN.	9:00am - 7:00pm

First opened 2017
Roaster For Five Coffee Roasters
Machine La Marzocco GB5 EE, 2 groups
Grinder Fiorenzato F64 EVO

Espresso	$3.00
Cappuccino	$4.25
Latte	$4.50

No. 170

Qathra Café

1112 Cortelyou Road, Brooklyn, NY 11218 | **Ditmas Park**

This Ditmas Park neighborhood shop has developed quite a following, and when you taste the coffee it's easy to see why. Despite its unassuming hand-painted decor (think 1990s Portland), Qathra is deadly serious about its coffee. Don't add milk to the excellent, robust Hario pour overs. If you do happen to be in the mood for something milky, indulge in a frothy, sweet latte. Snag a spot in the delightful backyard and start wondering why you haven't already moved to Brooklyn.

(347) 305-3250
www.qathra.nyc
Subway Q (Cortelyou Rd)

MON-SUN. 7:00am - 7:00pm

First opened 2010
Roaster Café Integral
Machine La Marzocco Strada MP, 3 groups
Grinder Mazzer Luigi Robur E

Espresso $2.50
Cappuccino $3.50
Latte $4.00

No. 171

Roots Cafe

639a 5th Avenue, Brooklyn, NY 11215 | **Park Slope**

In many ways, walking into Roots Cafe feels like walking into someone's home. Along the walls hang quirky paintings, musical instruments, and bookshelves filled with the classics. The 'hominess' is not merely aesthetic; it is a quality that extends to the service. Walk through to the counter in the back and interact with the engaging baristas who serve excellent espresso-based beverages alongside a variety of breakfast and lunch sandwiches. If you're craving something sweet, be sure to try the salted caramel latte or peppermint mocha.

(929) 301-5535
www.rootsbrooklyn.com
Subway D, N, R, W (Prospect Ave)

MON-FRI. 7:00am - 5:00pm
SAT-SUN. 8:00am - 6:00pm

First opened 2008
Roaster Forty Weight Coffee Roasters
Machine La Marzocco Linea EE, 2 groups
Grinder Mahlkönig K30 Twin

Espresso $2.50
Cappuccino $3.50
Latte $4.00

No. 172

Stonefruit Espresso + Kitchen

1058 Bedford Avenue, Brooklyn, NY 11205 | **Bed-Stuy**

A major spot for Bed-Stuy, Stonefruit is a little slice of Los Angeles, in the best sense possible. It's a coffee shop, it's a florist, it's a candle and used-book shop, it's a restaurant that serves wine. Comfortable rope-swing chairs hang from the ceiling in this beautifully designed, light-filled space. The baristas are perfectionists at handling milk. The single-origin pour overs are delicious, but the flat white is even better. The matcha latte is just as good; it's hard to choose what to drink here because they get everything right.

(718) 230-4147
stonefruitespresso.com
Subway G (Bedford - Nostrand Ave)

MON-FRI.	7:30am - 6:00pm
SAT-SUN.	8:30am - 6:00pm

First opened 2015
Roaster Counter Culture Coffee
Machine La Marzocco GB5, 2 groups
Grinder Mahlkönig EK 43

Espresso	$3.00
Cappuccino	$4.00
Latte	$4.00

No. 173

Photo: Tyler Nix

With The Brooklyn Academy of Music in Fort Greene, the beautiful and historic Promenade along the water in Brooklyn Heights and all the fashionable shops and restaurants in Carroll Gardens and Cobble Hill, it's easy to wander a day away in Downtown Brooklyn. These largely residential areas are filled with beautiful tree-lined streets and quiet parks, and are known for being home to many of New York's greatest artists, writers and musicians.

Downtown Brooklyn

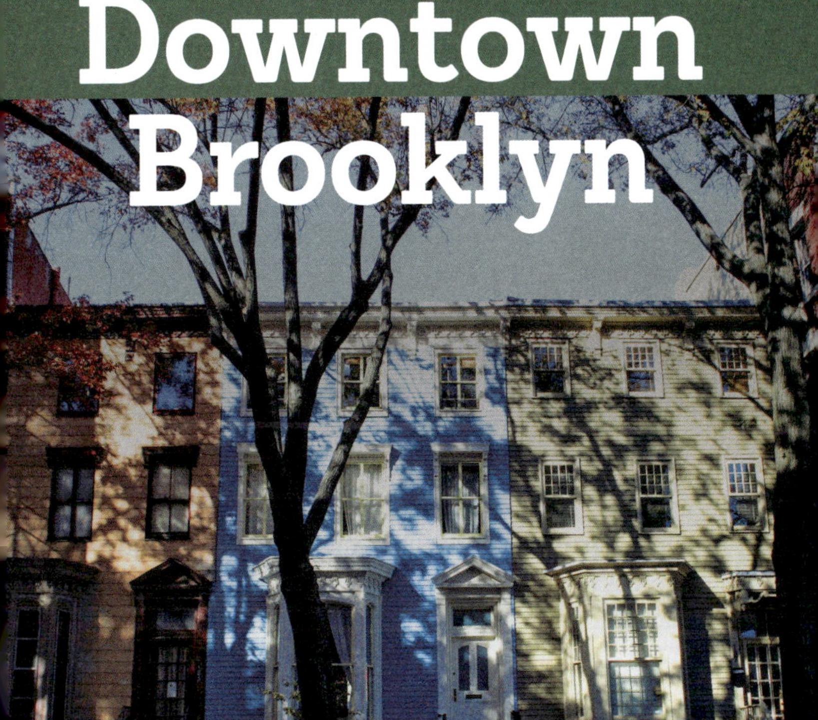

Black Star Bakery. Photo: Ben Hon

Abbotsford Road Coffee Specialists

573-577 Sackett Street, Brooklyn, NY 11217 | **Gowanus**

You know when a company is teaching other cafes how to do coffee, it's going to be good. Abbotsford Road has been supplying specialty beans and coffee education for decades, and their first and only outpost acts as a showroom for their incredible product. Their 'Crop to Cup' philosophy extends their community focus to ethical sourcing by building direct relationships with their growers. Co-owner Logan is hands-on in the roasting process, so make sure to ask about the beans on offer and try one of their fragrant pour overs. The cortado, too, is expertly pulled and the result is a beautifully balanced and sweet brew. Go for the education, return for the coffee.

(347) 384-2862
abbotsfordroad.com
Subway R (Union St)

MON-FRI. 8:00am - 3:00pm
SAT-SUN. 9:00am - 3:00pm

First opened 2017
Roaster Abbotsford Road Coffee Specialists
Machine Rancilio, 2 groups
Grinder Mazzer Luigi Major E, Mahlkönig EK 43

Espresso	$3.00
Cappuccino	$4.00
Latte	$4.00

No. 174

BKG Coffee Roasters

557 Myrtle Avenue, Brooklyn, NY 11205 | **Clinton Hill**

In 2006, the three Farrelly brothers from Bay Ridge Brooklyn - an engineer, a banker and a high school drop-out - opened a roastery in Red Hook. Before long, they were serving high profile clients like Facebook, and opening this quiet, unassuming neighborhood shop. An impressive 40% of their beans come from farmers they have a direct relationship with. Go for a single origin pour over, or the ultra-strong but somehow still sweet and silky cold brew. BKG features a lovely backyard which fills up with students from the nearby Pratt Institute.

www.bkgcoffee.com
Subway G (Classon Ave)

MON-SAT. 7:00am - 6:00pm
SUN. 8:00am - 6:00pm

First opened 2014
Roaster BKG Coffee Roasters
Machine Victoria Arduino White Eagle
Grinder Mahlkönig, Mazzer Luigi

Espresso	$3.25
Cappuccino	$4.00
Latte	$4.25

No. **175**

Bluestone Lane Dumbo

55 Prospect Street, Brooklyn, NY 11201 | **Dumbo**

Part of the new Dumbo Heights campus, Bluestone Lane goes all-out in its impressive first foray into Brooklyn. Upon entering this sophisticated cafe, it feels so similar yet so different from other Bluestone Lane locations all at once. Similar: the seafoam green tiles and light wood aesthetic that forms Bluestone Lane's brand identity - and of course the superb Aussie-inspired coffee. Different: a white marble bar and polished concrete flooring. Like its Manhattan cafes, the all-day menu focuses on seasonal offerings, and the avocado smash is their signature.

(718) 374-6858
bluestonelane.com
Subway F (York St) or A, C (High St)

MON-SUN. 7:30am - 6:30pm

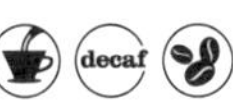

First opened 2016
Roaster Bluestone Lane
Machine La Marzocco Linea, 3 groups
Grinder Mazzer Luigi Robur E

Espresso	$3.20
Cappuccino	$4.25
Latte	$4.25

Sister locations Multiple locations

No. **176**

Brooklyn Roasting Company Dumbo

25 Jay Street, Brooklyn, NY 11201 | **Dumbo**

Brooklyn's flagship Navy Yard branch is a big, bustling operation that packs in customers of just about every age. Hipsters abound, but so do toddlers. This is one thing that makes the place so lively. Brooklyn Roasting Company offers a large and varied food menu and a good selection of non-caffeinated drinks such as fresh juices, and smoothies. But the coffee is the real star here, whether well-made milky drinks or daily brewed coffees (a changing selection) from excellent single-origin beans.

(718) 514-2874
www.brooklynroasting.com
Subway F (York St)

Sister locations Multiple locations

MON-SUN. 7:00am - 7:00pm

First opened 2011
Roaster Brooklyn Roasting Company
Machine La Marzocco GB5, 2 groups
Grinder Bunn

Espresso	$2.75
Cappuccino	$4.00
Latte	$4.50

No. 177

Coffee Project New York Brooklyn

78 Rockwell Place, Brooklyn, NY 11217 | **Fort Greene**

In the new wave of coffee fanaticism, attention to tasting notes rivals that of the wine industry. A visit to Coffee Project NY will have you feeling like an expert in no time. Their expansion to Brooklyn has introduced patrons to some of the most advanced brewing technology in the world of coffee, including Steampunk and Ground Control machines that use vacuum technology to extract 'delicate' notes in the brewing process. Female owners Chisum and Kaleena have been able to foster creativity and discovery in their team, allowing the space to function as a playground for baristas and a show for patrons. Once a month, staff are encouraged to create a new beverage to be featured in-store.

The 1,000 square foot space features a Slow Bar, a laptop-free counter serving pour-overs for an interactive experience, which offers an excellent opportunity to sample some of their rotating selection of beans. This demonstration area, complete with beakers and unfamiliar brews, may have the air of a science lab, but the 19-foot-high ceilings, exposed wood pylons, raw wood shared tables and textural crockery bring the cafe back down to earth. Paired with enthusiastic staff who are ready to share their expertise, this cafe has won over our hearts and minds.

No. 178

MON-FRI.	7:00am - 6:00pm
SAT.	8:00am - 6:00pm
SUN.	8:00am - 5:00pm

First opened 2018
Roaster Coffee Collective
Machine Synesso MVP Hydra, 3 groups
Grinder Mahlkönig Peak, Mahlkönig EK 43

Espresso	$3.25
Cappuccino	$4.25
Latte	$4.75

(585) 888-3153
www.coffeeprojectny.com
Subway 2, 3, 4, 5 (Nevins St)

Sister locations East Village

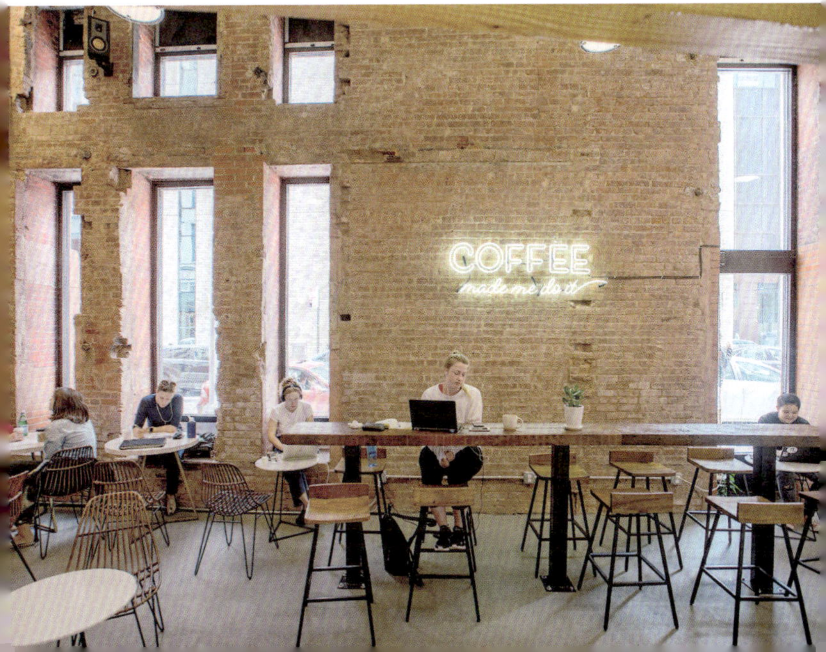

Devoción Downtown Brooklyn

276 Livingston Street, Brooklyn, NY 11201 | **Boerum Hill**

Entering Devoción feels like walking into an exotic hotel lobby. Generous in size, warm with natural light and accented with mismatched woods and vibrant yellow tiles (on brand, of course), it feels like summer all year around. In the heart of the space is a native plant life centerpiece which leads you around to the bar to watch a display of unique drip brewing methods and lovingly made pour overs. It's a perfect space to enjoy a freshly baked guava croissant, sip on exceptional coffee and be transported from New York straight to the fields of Colombia.

(718) 285-6180
www.devocion.com
Subway L (Bedford Ave)

Sister locations Williamsburg / Flatiron

MON-FRI.	7:00am - 7:00pm
SAT-SUN.	8:00am - 7:00pm

First opened 2018
Roaster Devoción
Machine Slayer Steam, 3 groups
Grinder Ceado E37K

Espresso	$3.50
Cappuccino	$4.50
Latte	$5.00

No. 179

East One Coffee Roasters Court Street

384 Court Street, Brooklyn, NY 11231 | **Carroll Gardens**

Coffee connoisseurs will fall in love with East One Coffee Roasters (E1), a hip venue in Carroll Gardens. Located on a lovely corner spot, this venue is striking in both the atmosphere and the quality of the roast. In addition to the spacious cafe up front, there is a large restaurant with a full-service menu - and trust us you do not want to skip it! The food is absolutely delicious, their beans are well roasted, and there is plenty of space to enjoy yourself with family and friends.

(347) 987-4919
www.eastonecoffee.com
Subway F, G (Carroll St)

Sister locations Baxter St / Chelsea

MON-SUN. 7:00am - 7:00pm
SAT-SUN. 8:00am - 7:00pm

First opened 2017
Roaster East One Coffee Roasters
Machine Slayer Steam, 3 groups
Grinder Mahlkönig Peak, Mahlkönig EK 43, Nuova Simonelli Mythos

Espresso $3.25
Cappuccino $4.25
Latte $4.50

No. 180

Kaigo Coffee Room

139 Bridge Park Drive Suite H4, Brooklyn, NY 11201 | **Brooklyn Heights**

Tucked between piers at Brooklyn Bridge Park, Kaigo Coffee Room may have the most peaceful view of any coffee shop in the city. The cafe's glass exterior offers an impressive outlook of the river and spectacle of the lower Manhattan skyline, making Kaigo the perfect place to sip and chill. After taking a minute to admire the mesmerizing mural occupying one of the interior walls, hand-painted by local artist Lauren Elizabeth Lee and designed to evoke owner Ivan's concept of the farm-to-cup process, your eyes are inevitably drawn to the equally attractive coffee menu. Beans from La Colombe and Onyx Coffee Lab are carefully handled to create offerings tending well beyond espresso-based brews.

Opt for one of the three consciously selected market pour-overs to have the perfect, seasonal coffee crafted before your eyes. If it's refreshment you're after, La Colombe cold brew is on tap and pairs perfectly with a stroll around Brooklyn Bridge Park, but Kaigo truly shines with their perfect milk texturing and latte art, so if you're craving silky milk, lean in.

No. 181

MON-SUN. 7:30am - 7:00pm

First opened 2018
Roaster Onyx Coffee Lab, La Colombe Coffee Roasters
Machine La Marzocco Strada AV, 3 groups
Grinder Mahlkönig Peak

Espresso	$3.50
Cappuccino	$4.50
Latte	$5.00

(347) 529-6180
www.kaigocoffee.com
Subway R, W (Court St) or 2, 3, 4, 5 (Borough Hall)

Sister locations Soho

Public Records

223 Butler Street, Brooklyn, NY 11217 | **Gowanus**

Cool, airy and raw, this whitewashed landmark structure provides the perfect canvas for this multi-purpose space. Public Records is a haven for audiophiles, hosting a hi-fi listening bar showcasing rare record collections, a "sound room" featuring live music and vinyl-centric DJs, and an all-day cafe and independent magazine shop curated by Import. The cafe works with local roasters Sey Coffee and the food and beverage menus are entirely vegan, paying homage to the building's history, formerly housing Brooklyn's ASPCA. Their celebration of music, independent and local sourcing, community building, and commitment to quality has us celebrating, too.

publicrecords.nyc
Subway N, Q, R, 2, 3, 4, 5 (Atlantic Ave - Barclays Center)

MON.	Closed
TUE-SUN.	9:00am - 5:00pm

First opened 2019
Roaster Sey Coffee Roasters
Machine La Marzocco GB5, 2 groups
Grinder Mahlkönig Peak, Mahlkönig EK 43

Espresso	$2.50
Cappuccino	$4.00
Latte	$4.50

No. 182

Relationships NYC

920 Fulton Street, Brooklyn, NY 11238 | **Clinton Hill**

Relationships offers a unique opportunity to enjoy Parlor Coffee in one of the most visually stimulating cafe-slash spaces in Brooklyn, which merges coffee, art, and design. Impeccably fresh, Relationships is a convivial design showroom providing an experiential setting to interact with a rotating selection of international and local curiosities. Owners Nina and Su bring fresh enthusiasm and a keen eye for detail through the entire cafe experience, from bean selection, cup, foaming and pouring of milk, to the flawless selection of unique local pastries from Saraghini, Roberta's and Clementine bakeries. We think this relationship will last.

(917) 909-1651
relationshipsnyc.com
Subway C (Clinton - Washington Aves)

MON-FRI. 7:00am - 5:00pm
SAT-SUN. 8:30am - 7:00pm

First opened 2018
Roaster Parlor Coffee
Machine La Marzocco Linea PB, 2 groups
Grinder Nuova Simonelli Mythos One

Espresso	$3.75
Cappuccino	$4.25
Latte	$4.75

No. 183

Stumptown Coffee Roasters Cobble Hill

212b Pacific Street, Brooklyn, NY 11201 | **Cobble Hill**

This Portland-based roastery has brought together a myriad of skilled designers and artists to reinvigorate an 1860s Brooklyn firehouse. The result is three cohesive zones, each with a different feel, to fit every guest's mood. Be welcomed by an enclosed garden front patio for caffeine hounds and regular hounds. Get comfortable in an art-filled back lounge with ample banquettes for those with a laptop in tow. Or, hang out in the grand cafe's buzzing center, where you can watch your morning coffee be prepared by an effortlessly cool member of the Stumptown family on one of the most beautiful La Marzocco machines we have ever seen. The Linea PB has been impeccably customized by Pantechnicon and delicately hand-painted by Melanie Nead, creating a porcelain effect and completely unique form.

The atmosphere is surprisingly intimate for such a large cafe, and with rotating records and a water station with sparkling water on tap, generosity springs to mind, in action and space. The pastry selection here shouldn't be looked past with Supermoon, DU's donuts and Ovenly baked goods on offer, and neither should the full menu of Mex-Californian bites by Lalito. The cafe's drinks menu includes a standard battery of established Stumptown offerings, including cold brew on tap and pour over drinks, with every bean sourced from direct trade relationships all over the world, all brought together under artist Zachary Marvick's custom ceiling tiles.

No. 184

MON-SUN. 7:00am - 7:00pm

First opened 2018
Roaster Stumptown Coffee Roasters
Machine La Marzocco Linea PB, 3 groups
Grinder Mazzer Luigi Robur E

Espresso	$3.25
Cappuccino	$4.00
Latte	$4.50

(347) 416-6741
www.stumptowncoffee.com
Subway 2, 3 (Borough Hall) or G, F (Bergen St)

Sister locations Grenwich Village / Ace Hotel

Photo: Caffe Vita (Lower East Side)

In the northern part of Brooklyn, Bushwick is fast becoming one of the most sought after neighborhoods. Spilling over from trendy Williamsburg, cafes, restaurants and boutiques are all finding new spots to feature their expanding retail offerings. With the addition of neighboring Bed-Stuy this area now has even more to enjoy.

Bushwick & Surrounding

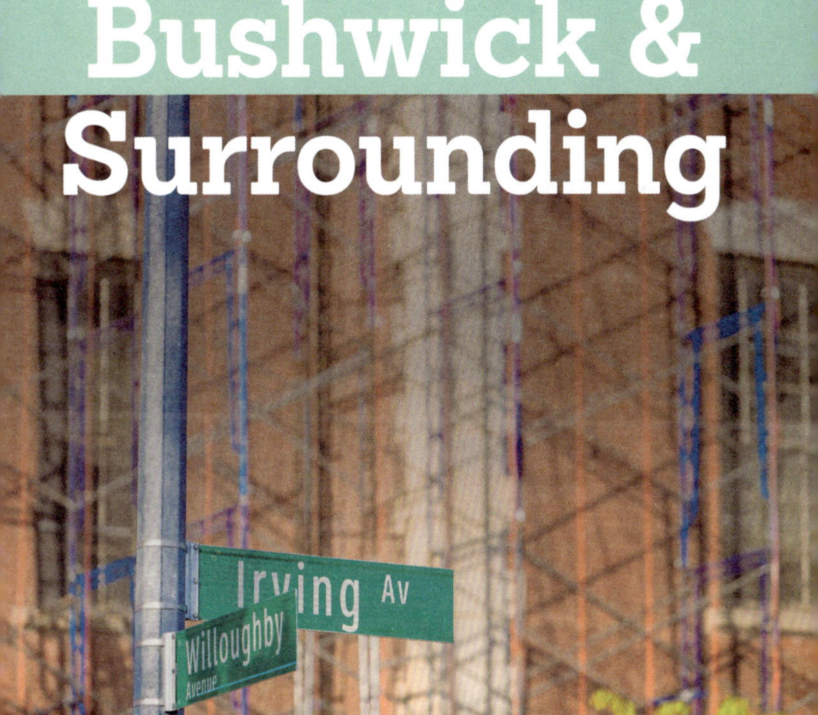

Photo: Ben Hider

AP Café: A Place Creative

420 Troutman Street, Brooklyn, NY 11237 | **Bushwick**

AP Café is a beautifully minimalist space that lets its fine coffee and food take focus within its vast, white-washed walls. The shop is bright, fresh, and the perfect spot to grab a drink and partake in its extensive menu of food offerings, ranging from quinoa bowls to freshly prepared seasonal juices. The coffee comes from Partners, and the menu features specialty drinks like Vietnamese iced coffee.

(347) 404-6147
www.apcafenyc.com
Subway L (Jefferson St)

MON-FRI. 8:00am - 6:00pm
SAT-SUN. 9:00am - 7:00pm

First opened 2013
Roaster Partners Coffee
Machine Faema E61 Legend, 2 groups
Grinder Mazzer Luigi

Espresso $2.99
Cappuccino $3.81
Latte $4.36

No. 185

Baby Skips

1158 Myrtle Avenue, Brooklyn, NY 11221 | **Bushwick**

Baby Skips, the adorable younger sibling of the now-closed Little Skips, is an oasis in Bushwick. Yes, it is smaller than the original (hence the name), but what it lacks in size it makes up for in atmosphere - and you can always find a seat. Friendly baristas serve Counter Culture coffee with great enthusiasm - stop by a handful of times and they will almost certainly remember your order. Pair your morning latte with one of their delicious pastries, which are as fresh as you can get. We love you Baby Skips!

(929) 210-8101
littleskips.nyc
Subway M, J, Z (Myrtle Ave)

Sister locations Little Skips East

MON-FRI. 7:00am - 6:00pm
SAT-SUN. 8:00am - 6:00pm

First opened 2014
Roaster Counter Culture Coffee, City of Saints Coffee Roasters
Machine La Marzocco GB5
Grinder Mazzer Luigi Robur E

Espresso	$3.00
Cappuccino	$4.00
Latte	$4.25

No. 186

Caffe Vita Coffee Roasting Co. Bushwick

576 Johnson Avenue, Brooklyn, NY 11237 | **Bushwick**

Right in the still-industrial heart of old Bushwick, Caffe Vita's roastery/cafe has plenty of seating and a bird's eye view of the roaster in action. The Vita folks buy beans direct from producers, something they championed at an early stage in Third Wave coffee history, and they put the product to great use. In addition to expertly-made pour over and espresso-based drinks, you shouldn't miss out on their sweetened take on nitro-brewed cold brew, as well as their unconventional rolls.

(929) 295-9328
www.caffevita.com
Subway L (Jefferson St)

Sister locations Lower East Side

MON-SUN. 7:00am - 6:00pm

First opened 2015
Roaster Caffe Vita Coffee Roasting Co.
Machine Kees van der Westen Spirit, 3 groups
Grinder Mazzer Luigi Robur E

Espresso	$3.50
Cappuccino	$4.75
Latte	$5.00

No. 187

City of Saints Coffee Roasters Bushwick Cafe & Roastery

297 Meserole Street, Brooklyn, NY 11206 | **Bushwick**

The industrial part of Bushwick is full of warehouses, many of which are being converted into trendy businesses and fancy apartments. Refreshingly, City of Saints still feels very much like a warehouse, with its corrugated metal pull-down door entrance and a beautiful graffiti mural decorating one of its walls. This is where City of Saints roast their beans - in full view, if you're curious to watch - with a few cafe tables in front. Their excellent coffee bar always has a constantly rotating selection to tempt you, but for an ultimate palate experience, the cold brew is the one to try.

(929) 900-5282
www.cityofsaintscoffee.com
Subway L (Montrose Ave)

MON-FRI. 7:00am - 6:00pm
SAT-SUN. 8:00am - 5:00pm

First opened 2015
Roaster City of Saints Coffee Roasters
Machine Victoria Arduino Black Eagle, 2 groups
Grinder Nuova Simonelli Mythos Clima Pro

Espresso	$3.00
Cappuccino	$4.25
Latte	$4.75

Sister locations Astor Cafe

No. 188

Dweebs

1434 DeKalb Avenue, Brooklyn, NY 11237 | **Bushwick**

Coffee geekery at its finest: Good coffee, good people, and zero pretension.
In contrast to its name, the interior is inherently cool with full albums on rotation, a wall dedicated to projected videos, monthly rotating local art installations, and a food and drink menu painted directly onto the wall near the cafe's entrance. Owners Will and Mike intend the cafe to be inclusive and aspire to create a passion for coffee in their customer base. The full house shows it's working. When he isn't behind the machine, Will also works for Spectrum Coffee, bringing along expert supply chain knowledge to Dweebs' precise selection of lighter roast beans fresh from harvest. Visit to chill out, geek out, or both.

MON-SUN. 7:00am - 7:00pm

First opened 2015
Roaster Spectrum Coffees
Machine Synesso MVP Hydra, 2 groups
Grinder Mahlkönig K30, Mahlkönig EK 43

Espresso	$3.00
Cappuccino	$3.50
Latte	$4.00

(347) 452-9728
www.dweebsbk.com
Subway L (DeKalb Ave)

No. 189

Milk & Pull Bushwick

181 Irving Avenue, Brooklyn, NY 11237 | **Bushwick**

Milk & Pull couldn't be a more unassuming local, nestled in a quiet block in Bushwick with just a few seats outside and a modest frontage. But it's a wonderful place, with a long, narrow, brightly-painted interior and a tempting array of baked goodies to ogle while waiting for your coffee, which is exceptionally well made. Stumptown beans are treated royally on the La Marzocco and there is great latte art even on a macchiato. Milk & Pull has a solid core of regulars; you'll see why they keep on coming back.

(347) 627-8511
www.milkandpull.com
Subway L (DeKalb Ave)

Sister locations Ridgewood / Bed-Stuy

MON-FRI.	7:00am - 6:00pm
SAT.	8:00am - 6:00pm
SUN.	8:00am - 5:00pm

First opened 2013
Roaster Stumptown Coffee Roasters
Machine La Marzocco Linea, 2 groups
Grinder Mazzer Luigi Robur E

Espresso	$3.27
Cappuccino	$3.50
Latte	$4.37

No. 190

Milk & Pull Ridgewood

778 Seneca Avenue, Queens, NY 11385 | **Ridgewood**

This Ridgewood outpost of Milk & Pull brings well-made coffee to this burgeoning neighborhood. The menu features coffee from Portland star roaster Stumptown with espressos and cold brew, a standard for serious cafes today. They prepare fresh sandwiches and bagels and offer a nice variety of local baked goods. Exposed brick and natural wood make up the bright, airy place that features large tables spread leisurely apart, allowing for plenty of space to sit and relax.

(718) 821-1155
www.milkandpull.com
Subway M (Seneca Ave)

Sister locations Bushwick / Bed-Stuy

MON-FRI.	7:00am - 7:00pm
SAT.	8:00am - 7:00pm
SUN.	8:00am - 6:00pm

First opened 2015
Roaster Stumptown Coffee Roasters
Machine La Marzocco GB5, 2 groups
Grinder Mazzer Luigi Kony

Espresso	$3.00
Cappuccino	$4.00
Latte	$4.25

Sey Coffee

18 Grattan Street, Brooklyn, NY 11206 | **East Williamsburg**

Sey Coffee is the epitome of what a Brooklyn coffee shop should be; an open, relaxed, and inviting space in which excellent coffee can be found. The cafe is delightful, spacious and modern, accented with dozens of potted plants and a large garage door that is thrown open in the summer months. The coffee is roasted directly behind their shop, meaning it's served exactly as the roasters intended it to be. The meticulous baristas ensure that everything, from an espresso to a pour over, is treated with care and attention, providing a wonderful drinking experience. Needless to Sey, this place is a must-visit for any coffee-loving New Yorker.

MON-FRI. 7:00am - 7:00pm
SAT-SUN. 8:00am - 7:00pm

First opened 2017
Roaster Sey Coffee
Machine La Marzocco Linea PB, 2 groups
Grinder Mahlkönig Peak, Mahlkönig EK 43

Espresso	$4.50
Cappuccino	$5.00
Latte	$6.00

(347) 871-1611
seycoffee.com
Subway L (Morgan Ave)

No. 192

Variety Coffee Roasters Bushwick

146 Wyckoff Avenue, Brooklyn, NY 11237 | **Bushwick**

Any place where you can play Ms Pac Man on a real arcade table has got to be legendary, and this big Variety flagship boasts exactly that. But it's not all fun and games here, as plenty of people sit and work. The décor is dominated by white paint, dark wood and exposed brick. The coffee offering is Variety's usual high-class stuff, brewed by experts using beans roasted at the back of the room. Service is swift and friendly, and you can get plenty of sound advice about what to drink.

(718) 497-2326
varietycoffeeroasters.com
Subway L (DeKalb Ave)

Sister locations Greenpoint / Williamsburg / Chelsea / Upper East Side

MON-SUN. 7:00am - 9:00pm

First opened 2014
Roaster Variety Coffee Roasters
Machine La Marzocco Linea PB, 3 groups
Grinder Mahlkönig Peak

Espresso	$3.00
Cappuccino	$4.00
Latte	$4.50

No. 193

Williamsburg

194 Blue Bottle Coffee (Williamsburg) p215
195 Charter Coffeehouse p216
196 Devoción (Williamsburg) p217 ◊
197 Gimme! Coffee (Williamsburg) p218
198 Hardwater Coffee Co. p219 *
199 JANE Motorcycles p221
200 Mountain Province p222 *
201 Oslo Coffee Roasters (Williamsburg) p223
202 Partners Coffee (Williamsburg) p224 ◊
203 Sweatshop p225 ◊
204 Tar Pit p226
205 Upstate Stock p226

* NEW	◊ TOP 40	◊ TOP 10

Williamsburg

Williamsburg is a popular, trendy neighborhood with a lively, youthful feel. This area is a mecca for foodies, featuring lots of coffee roasteries housed in its converted warehouses, the Smorgasburg food market on the waterfront in the summertime and plenty of exciting restaurants. It's also home to a range of vintage shops, art galleries, music venues and McCarren Park on its northern edge.

Blue Bottle Coffee Williamsburg

76 North 4th Street, Brooklyn, NY 11249 | **Williamsburg**

Through the glass exterior on North 4th, the newest addition to the Blue Bottle empire - with its familiar coastal California aesthetic - sinks down from the street, providing an impeccable view of the generously sized location. Inside, a growing line of coffee lovers snakes through the curved, motion driven architecture. The ability to select from a seasonal variety of beans for pour overs and the wide array of preparations on full display across the counter provide an experience of ordering to match the delights of the coffee itself. However, the location's streamlined entry and exit points, combined with an absence of WiFi, do create more of a takeaway vibe, but there is also plenty of seating, so soak in the scene while you can.

(510) 653-3394
bluebottlecoffee.com
Subway L (Bedford Ave)

MON-FRI. 6:30am - 7:00pm
SAT-SUN. 7:00am - 7:30pm

First opened 2017
Roaster Blue Bottle Coffee
Machine La Marzocco Linea PB, 3 groups
Grinder Baratza Forté, Mazzer Luigi

Espresso $3.50
Cappuccino $4.50
Latte $5.00

Sister locations Multiple locations

No. 194

Charter Coffeehouse

309 Graham Avenue, Brooklyn, NY 11211 | **Williamsburg**

Serving up expertly brewed coffee, Charter Coffeehouse is a cozy, compact 20-seater cafe in the heart of Williamsburg. Raw and reused wood make for a quirky, laid back edge. The owners, Scott Cameron & Chrissy Tsang, have set out not only to deliver fantastic coffee, but also to support the people behind the beans by donating 5% of all profits to help the development of the coffee farming communities. And as if all of that wasn't reason enough to visit, Chrissy has a background in hair-cutting, and she practices her art out back. Sip and snip anyone?

(347) 721-3735
chartercoffee.com
Subway L (Graham Ave)

MON-FRI. 7:00am - 7:00pm
SAT-SUN. 8:00am - 7:00pm

First opened 2016
Roaster Multiple roasters
Machine La Marzocco Linea PB EE, 2 groups
Grinder Nuova Simonelli Mythos Clima Pro, Mahlkönig EK 43

Espresso	$3.50
Cappuccino	$4.50
Latte	$4.75

No. 195

Devoción Williamsburg

69 Grand Street, Brooklyn, NY 11249 | **Williamsburg**

Williamsburg

You can enjoy the world's finest artisan Colombian coffees here at this sprawling cafe, as Devoción sources and purchases all their coffee from Colombia. The shop reflects this focus with its spectacular space, outfitted with its roastery in the front where you can see the roasters hard at work. The main room is an impressive chamber, bursting with sun from a center skylight. The space is huge, with plenty of tables and deliciously sunken-in couches, accented by an incredible living wall, with impressive plants all native to Colombia.

(718) 285-6180
www.devocion.com
Subway J, Z (Marcy Ave) or L (Bedford Ave) or G (Metropolitan Ave)

MON-FRI. 7:00am - 7:00pm
SAT-SUN. 8:00am - 7:00pm

First opened 2014
Roaster Devoción
Machine La Marzocco Leva, 3 groups
Grinder Ceado E37K

Espresso $3.50
Cappuccino $4.50
Latte $5.00

Sister locations Downtown Brooklyn / Flatiron District

No. 196

Gimme! Coffee Williamsburg

495 Lorimer Street, Brooklyn, NY 11211 | **Williamsburg**

Gimme! Coffee's unassuming design might fool you into thinking that this is just another nice neighborhood coffee joint. In reality it's a decade-and-a-half old branch of an Ithica based roaster that's as serious about the expertise of its baristas as it is the ethics by which they procure their beans. While they meticulously prepare your delicately-flavored pour over, an amiable barista might tell you about new equipment the farmers purchased with funding provided by Gimme!

(718) 388-7771
gimmecoffee.com
Subway L (Lorimer St) or G (Metropolitan Ave)

MON-SUN. 7:00am - 6:00pm

First opened 2004
Roaster Gimme! Coffee
Machine La Marzocco Linea, 2 groups
Grinder Mazzer Luigi, Bunn

Espresso $3.25
Cappuccino $4.75
Latte $4.75

Sister locations Nolita

No. 197

Hardwater Coffee Co.

340 Bedford Avenue, Brooklyn, NY 11249 | **Williamsburg**

Crisp, concise, and hard design provides the foundation for this new and very welcome addition to South Williamsburg. Hardwater Coffee Co.'s minimalist aesthetic is defined mainly by off-white tiled floors, black furnishings and an abundance of cacti, creating a bright, clean and welcoming space. Casual bar seating a offers a perfect perch for laptopping, particularly on warmer days when the front windows are opened onto Bedford Avenue. Keep on walking past the black and white skull icons behind the counter to discover their generous backyard patio with chill California vibes, which pairs perfectly with a cold brew. In a neighborhood where third-party coffee and fighting for a seat is rife, their focus on small-batch, locally roasted coffee and providing ample space where people can hang out makes this cafe a standout.

Hardwater's signature FIEND blend is expertly pulled and lends itself perfectly to any espresso-and-milk drink, but opt for a cortado to truly appreciate its creamy and chocolatey, yet berry-crisp profile. Balthazar pastries are delivered daily, and their full-service kitchen offers a breakfast and lunch menu, so you can stay for hours and enjoy fresh food along with some seriously good coffee.

No. 198

MON-FRI. 7:00am - 6:00pm
SAT-SUN. 8:00am - 7:00pm

First opened 2019
Roaster Hardwater Coffee Co.
Machine La Marzocco Linea EE, 2 groups
Grinder Mahlkönig Peak

Espresso $3.75
Cappuccino $4.50
Latte $4.50

www.hardwatercoffee.com
Subway J, M (Marcy Ave) or
L (Bedford Ave)

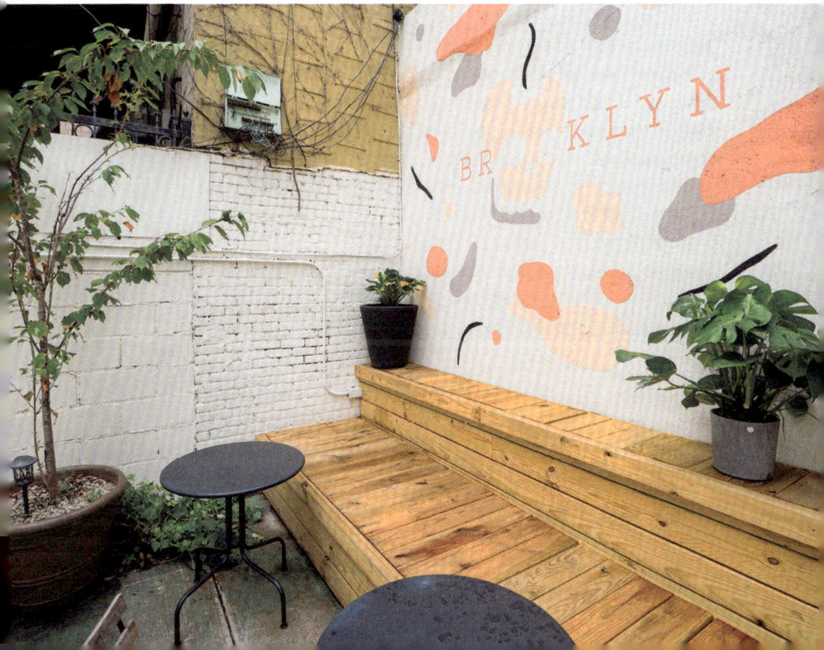

JANE Motorcycles

396 Wythe Avenue, Brooklyn, NY 11249 | **Williamsburg**

JANE Motorcycles is the one-stop-shop for all of your bike (and coffee!) needs. Serving up Counter Culture Coffee, a staple Brooklyn roaster, and all the motorcycle related attire one could hope for, JANE Motorcycles is truly a gem in the Williamsburg coffee scene. Grab your cup of joe in the front before browsing the gear. The well-designed shop is bright, airy, and easy on the eye. Whether you're a biker or not, ride on in for the coffee alone; it's well worth the visit.

(347) 844-9075
janemotorcycles.com
Subway J, M, Z (Marcy Ave)

MON-FRI. 7:00am - 7:00pm
SAT-SUN. 8:00am - 7:00pm

First opened 2013
Roaster Counter Culture Coffee
Machine La Marzocco Linea, 2 groups
Grinder Mazzer Luigi

Espresso $3.00
Cappuccino $4.00
Latte $4.50

No. 199

Mountain Province

9 Meserole Street, Brooklyn, NY 11211 | **East Williamsburg**

NEW

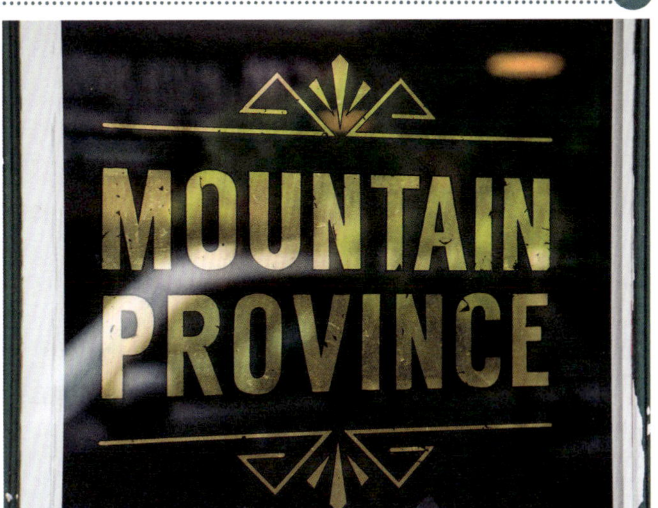

Mountain Province stands out from the sea of 'hip' coffee shops in the neighborhood for looking like a Filipino grandma's house, and we're loving it. Faded palm tree wallpaper, antique cabinets, and assorted chairs instantly provide a feeling of comfort and ease, only enhanced by welcoming smiles from the family behind the coffee machine. Sourcing their organic, fair trade, single-origin beans from the Mountain Provinces in the Philippines, their coffee is unique and lovingly pulled. Pick a chair and enjoy alongside taro and purple yam brioche, cassava cake, and pineapple scones, all baked in-house in celebration of owner Ray Luna's Filipino elders.

(718) 387-7030
www.mountainprovincecoffee.com
Subway G (Broadway) or J, M, Z (Lorimer St)

MON-FRI.	7:00am - 7:00pm
SAT-SUN.	8:00am - 6:00pm

First opened 2013
Roaster Kalsada Coffee
Machine La Marzocco Linea EE, 2 groups
Grinder Mazzer Luigi

Espresso	$3.00
Cappuccino	$4.25
Latte	$4.50

No. 200

Oslo Coffee Roasters Williamsburg

133b Roebling Street, Brooklyn, NY 11211 | **Williamsburg**

Away from the hub of Williamsburg's eat/drink/shop district, but close enough for easy access, this branch of Oslo is a fantastic place to while away the hours. You'll look through big windows fronting the high-ceilinged corner room, with fellow drinkers ranging from solitary workers to lively family groups. The coffee is roasted nearby, from beans bought through direct trade and sold as three house blends. Lovingly brewed into some of New York City's best cups, this Oslo outpost is a destination in its own right.

(718) 782-0332
oslocoffee.com
Subway L (Bedford Ave)

Sister locations Upper East Side / Williamsburg

MON-FRI.	7:00am - 7:00pm
SAT-SUN.	8:00am - 7:00pm (6:00pm in winter)

First opened 2003
Roaster Oslo Coffee Roasters
Machine Synesso Cyncra, 3 groups
Grinder Mazzer Luigi Major

Espresso	$3.25
Cappuccino	$4.25
Latte	$4.25

No. **201**

Partners Coffee Williamsburg

125 North 6th Street, Brooklyn, NY 11249 | **Williamsburg**

Photo: Kathryn Sheldon for Partners Coffee

Williamsburg wasn't complete until Partners (previously Toby's Estate) came to town. Everything on the menu (both beverage and food) is worth making the trip for, but go for the bright, single-origin espresso, straight up. Trust us, there really is a difference between this and the house blend espresso, especially fresh as the beans are roasted in front of you. Partners' near-flawlessness extends to the friendly, efficient service and the stylish, comfortable, loft-reminiscent design - which is often mobbed with laptops. Before you go, you also have to try the signature flat white, so smooth and rich it takes you to another world.

(347) 457-6160
www.partnerscoffee.com
Subway L (Bedford Ave)

MON-SUN. 6:30am - 7:00pm

First opened 2012
Roaster Partners Coffee
Machine La Marzocco Linea PB, 4 groups
Grinder Nuova Simonelli Mythos One Clima Pro, Mahlkönig Peak

Espresso $3.25
Cappuccino $4.00
Latte $4.75

Sister locations Long Island City / West Village / Bushwick / Vanderbilt Market

Sweatshop

232 Metropolitan Avenue, Brooklyn, NY 11211 | **Williamsburg**

Australian-owned Sweatshop is full of things that'll make you smile, from the big neon Sweatshop sign to the 'Death Before Decaf' tote bags, to the hand-painted stool-tops. Smiles continue when you start sipping brews from the sleek La Marzocco espresso machine. The single-origin espresso from Counter Culture Coffee changes every one or two weeks, and latte and macchiato boast exquisite latte art. Food is simple but well executed, with healthy Aussie-style breakfasts giving way at lunch to 'jaffles'(toasted sandwiches). In the words of co-owner Luke, 'We do what we do back home and hope that people dig it.' Full seats both indoors and out suggest they do.

(917) 960-7232
sweatshop.coffee
Subway L (Bedford Ave)

MON-FRI. 7:00am - 6:00pm
SAT-SUN. 8:00am - 6:00pm

First opened 2014
Roaster Counter Culture Coffee
Machine La Marzocco FB80, 2 groups
Grinder Mahlkönig Peak, Mahlkönig EK 43

Espresso $3.00
Cappuccino $4.25
Latte $4.50

No. 203

Tar Pit

135 Woodpoint Road, Brooklyn, NY 11211 | **Williamsburg**

Tucked away on a residential block in Williamsburg, this best-kept-secret might be the most tranquil, cozy coffee experience in the city. Everything about Tar Pit feels handcrafted - the copper and wood-bric-a-brac-strewn space was designed by the owner, a motorcycle mechanic. The coffee is excellent, from the espresso to the two kinds of cold brew, to the pour overs (the drip, from Plowshares, is also single-origin). But treat yourself to a cortado - the milk, from Battenkill Creamery, is of such high quality and handled so delicately it's sweeter and smoother than most lattes you'll ever have.

(917) 705-8031
www.tarpitcafe.com
Subway L (Graham Ave)

MON-FRI. 7:00am - 7:00pm
SAT-SUN. 8:00am - 7:00pm

First opened 2011
Roaster Plowshares Coffee Roasters
Machine La Marzocco Linea MP, 2 groups
Grinder Mazzer Luigi Super Jolly E

Espresso $2.50
Cappuccino $3.75
Latte $4.00

No. **204**

Upstate Stock

2 Berry Street, Brooklyn, NY 11249 | **Williamsburg**

Almost too-Brooklyn-to-be-true, in the best possible sense, Upstate Stock is a store that sells a selection of home & beauty products, which happens to have a great coffee bar in the front with plenty of seating (a generous touch). Coffee from Sweetleaf is skilfully pulled from the Astoria machine, creating a wonderfully flavorful espresso. The campfire latte might sound gimmicky but it's essential - touched with delicious smoked maple syrup and sea salt, it truly smells and tastes like summer camp.

www.upstatestock.com
Subway G (Nassau Ave) or L (Bedford Ave)

MON-FRI. 8:00am - 6:00pm
SAT. 8:00am - 7:00pm
SUN. 9:00am - 6:00pm

First opened 2016
Roaster Sweetleaf Coffee Roasters
Machine Astoria Gloria
Grinder Mahlkönig

Espresso $3.00
Cappuccino $4.00
Latte $4.50

No. **205**

Photo: Ben Hider

Growing in popularity, the neighborhoods of Astoria, Long Island City and Greenpoint are hubs of culture, history and lots of good food. Greenpoint adjoins Williamsburg on the other side of McCarren Park and, although quiet, is full of innovative eateries and shops. Walk over Pulaski Bridge to Long Island City and explore a burgeoning part of Queens where lots of new restaurants, MoMA's contemporary art affiliate PS1 and a thriving creative community can be found. Astoria boasts a diverse cultural mix that includes Italian, Jewish and Greek communities.

Greenpoint & Queens

Astoria Coffee

30-04 30th Street, Queens, NY 11102 | **Astoria**

Astoria Coffee brings a special love for the glorious bean at this neighborhood shop, hosting a variety of different coffees here. They source from multiple American roasters, and have the beans available to purchase. They keep at least two different types of roasts on the bar for espresso drinks. Don't hesitate to ask questions because the baristas are more than happy to walk you through the tasting notes to get you just what you're looking for.

(347) 619-3915
www.astoriacoffeeny.com
Subway N, W (30th Ave)

MON-FRI. 7:00am - 7:00pm
SAT-SUN. 7:00am - 8:00pm

First opened 2014
Roaster Multiple roasters
Machine Synesso MVP Hydra, 2 groups
Grinder Mahlkönig EK 43, Compak E8, Compak E10

Espresso $3.00
Cappuccino $4.00
Latte $4.00

No. 206

Birch Coffee Long Island City

40-37 23rd Street, Queens, NY 11101 | **Long Island City**

You can't actually walk around the beautiful roastery here, but the views, scent, and sounds of it behind glass are exciting enough to bring out every coffee geek's inner child. You can't get beans any fresher than this, and you can taste it in every drink. The espresso is so intense that even the latte has a strong flavor. It's been said that what separates a good barista from a great barista is that a great barista throws out a lot of shots, and we've seen a barista throw out three shots before he felt it was worthy of being served, a testament to Birch's commitment to quality.

(212) 686-1444
www.birchcoffee.com
Subway F (21st St - Queensbridge)

Sister locations Multiple locations

MON-FRI.	7:30am - 4:00pm
SAT-SUN.	9:00am - 4:00pm

First opened 2015
Roaster Birch Coffee
Machine La Marzocco Linea, 2 groups
Grinder Mahlkönig K30 Twin

Espresso	$3.25
Cappuccino	$4.00
Latte	$4.50

No. 207

Café Grumpy Greenpoint

193 Meserole Avenue, Brooklyn, NY 11222 | **Greenpoint**

Café Grumpy's original location, in the quiet residential edge of Greenpoint, is so large and the clientele exude such laid-back artsiness that you get the sense you could bring in an easel and start painting a portrait, and no one would raise an eyebrow. Anyone can appreciate the frothy light texture of their latte, but Grumpy, who roast their own beans in the back, cater to coffee nerds. In addition to reliably delicate, rich pour overs (which really do get even more flavorful as they cool down), they offer a single-origin espresso in addition to a house blend.

(718) 349-7623
cafegrumpy.com
Subway G (Nassau Ave) or G (Greenpoint Ave)

Sister locations Multiple locations

MON-FRI.	7:00am - 7:30pm
SAT-SUN.	7:30am - 7:30pm

First opened 2005
Roaster Café Grumpy
Machine Synesso Cyncra, 2 groups
Grinder Nuova Simonelli Mythos One Clima Pro, Mahlkönig Guatemala

Espresso	$3.75
Cappuccino	$4.50
Latte	$5.00

No. 208

Champion Coffee

142 Nassau Avenue, Brooklyn, NY 11222 | **Greenpoint**

A small but powerful coffee bar at the far end of Greenpoint's Manhattan Avenue, this place makes for a particularly lovely visit when the weather is nice and the garden is open in the back. Champion roast their own coffee in Queens, and their signature espresso blend is not to be missed, rich with notes of bittersweet cocoa and beautiful in any milky drink. Pair your brew with a house-made avocado toast for a true breakfast of Champions!

(718) 383-5195
www.championcoffee.com
Subway G (Nassau Ave)

Sister locations Multiple locations

MON-SUN. 7:00am - 7:00pm

First opened 2014
Roaster Champion Coffee
Machine La Marzocco FB80, 2 groups
Grinder Mahlkönig K30

Espresso $3.00
Cappuccino $4.50
Latte $4.50

No. 209

Homecoming

107 Franklin Street, Brooklyn, NY 11222 | **Greenpoint**

Homecoming is a beautiful flower shop on this busy little stretch of Franklin Street that couples fresh fantastic coffees with their floral arrangements. They serve Heart coffee, as well as fine teas, made by charming baristas at this loveable shop. They have a carefully curated selection of home goods here as well, with handmade notebooks, soaps and pots for your plants. It's easy to imagine building your perfect home here, right down to the coffee on the table.

(347) 457-5385
home-coming.com
Subway G (Greenpoint Ave)

Sister locations Williamsburg

MON-FRI. 7:30am - 7:00pm
SAT-SUN. 8:30am - 7:00pm

First opened 2013
Roaster Heart Coffee Roasters
Machine La Marzocco Linea, 2 groups
Grinder Mazzer Luigi Robur

Espresso $3.25
Cappuccino $4.50
Latte $5.00

No. 210

Kinship Coffee

30-5 Steinway Street, Queens, NY 11103 | **Astoria**

Stumptown Coffee is served at this charming Astoria shop, but they also keep a rotating menu of seasonal single- and dual-origins from a variety of roasters. It's got fresh pastries from not one, not two, but three of the very best bakeries in the city, as well as specialty chocolates for good measure. Though the space is small, the shop is bright and has just enough leg room to be a local favorite.

Subway N, W (30th Ave)

Sister locations Steinway & Broadway / Broadway & 31st

MON-SAT.	7:00am - 8:00pm
SUN.	8:00am - 8:00pm

First opened 2014
Roaster Tandem Coffee, Heart Coffee Roasters, Stumptown Coffee Roasters
Machine Synesso Cyncra, 2 groups
Grinder Mahlkönig EK 43, Compak K10

Espresso	$3.25
Cappuccino	$4.00
Latte	$4.50

No. 211

The Mill

44-61 11th Street, Queens, NY 11101 | **Long Island City**

The Mill has continued to be a mainstay in the heart of Long Island City since 2017. A patchwork of wood, this cafe and roastery has a rustic and abundant feel, offering a variety of slow-brewed coffees and a custom three-bean blend as the base for all espresso drinks, roasted within the borough by For Five. These are served alongside wholesome house-made lunch and grab and go bites covering all dietary requirements. It only makes sense that mornings attract a line of caffeine addicts out the door. If there's no rush in your hour, sit, gather, recharge, and soak up some vinyl.

(718) 843 -6455
www.themillcoffeelic.com
Subway E, M (Jackson Ave)

MON-FRI. 6:30am - 6:00pm
SAT-SUN. 8:00am - 6:00pm

First opened 2014
Roaster The Mill
Machine La Marzocco Linea EE, 2 groups
Grinder Mazzer Luigi

Espresso $2.75
Cappuccino $3.50
Latte $4.00

No. 212

New York City Bagel & Coffee House

40-05 Broadway, Queens, NY 11103 | **Astoria**

You know how some places feel like they've been around forever? Little more than four years old in Astoria, NYC Bagel & Coffee House is one of them. People seem to feel at home here. They come for bagels, sure: outstanding specimens in two sizes (the 'mini' is plenty) with loads of interesting fillings. But also for the coffee and baked sweet goods including enticing donuts. Note: though there are no loyalty cards, 'familiar faces get a 'loyalty bonus.'' No wonder 50 per cent of customers are regulars.

(718) 728-9511
www.nycbch.com
Subway M, R (46th St)

Sister locations Long Island City / Astoria

MON-SUN. 6:00am - 9:00pm

First opened 2015
Roaster For Five Coffee Roasters
Machine La Marzocco FB80
Grinder Mazzer Luigi x2

Espresso	$2.15
Cappuccino	$3.65
Latte	$3.65

No. 213

Odd Fox Coffee

984 Manhattan Avenue, Brooklyn, NY 11222 | **Greenpoint**

Odd Fox doesn't deny that its name is a bit strange, but that's all part of the fun. Serving first rate products, including Palor coffee and Ovenly pastries, Odd Fox has established itself as a strong player in the Greenpoint coffee scene. Its low-key ambiance, soft lighting, and gentle music make it a great place to come with a book or your laptop (there are outlets next to every table!). Coffee connoisseurs, take the opportunity to chat with the friendly and knowledgeable baristas as they pull flavorful espressos.

oddfoxcoffee.com
Subway G (Greenpoint Ave)

MON-FRI. 7:00am - 7:00pm
SAT-SUN. 8:00am - 8:00pm

First opened 2016
Roaster Parlor Coffee Roasters
Machine La Marzocco Linea, 2 groups
Grinder Mazzer Luigi Robur E

Espresso $3.00
Cappuccino $4.00
Latte $4.00

Partners Coffee Long Island City

26-25 Jackson Avenue, Queens, NY 11101 | **Long Island City**

Photo: Kathryn Sheldon for Partners Coffee

This latest branch of Partners (formerly Toby's Estate) is one of the best, with the company's usual top-quality beans brewed beautifully whichever method you go for. Lovers of cold brew should check out their 'Black + White'; milky, slightly sweetened, totally addictive. The only thing that can make the coffee better is the space - an early 20th-century building that served as an art gallery in one of its earlier incarnations. The whole building has been hollowed out so the room goes right up into the roof, with massive steel and wooden beams and gorgeous lighting including contemporary-style chandeliers over the counter and main seating area. It's a little like being in a coffee cathedral.

(347) 531-0477
www.partnerscoffee.com
Subway E, G, M, 7 (Court Sq)

MON-SUN. 6:30am - 7:00pm

First opened 2017
Roaster Partners Coffee
Machine La Marzocco Strada EE, 3 groups
Grinder Mazzer Luigi Robur E

Espresso $3.25
Cappuccino $4.00
Latte $4.75

Sister locations Williamsburg / Bushwick / West Village / Vanderbilt Market

No. 215

Sweetleaf Coffee & Cocktails

Center Boulevard 4615 Center Boulevard, Queens, NY 11101 | **Long Island City**

Long Island City is a neighborhood full of very-recently-constructed buildings, but this outpost of Sweetleaf feels like it's been here for decades. At night it turns into a bar serving cocktails and American beers, but during the day it's perfect for parents with babies and freelancers tapping at laptops. True to its name, the espresso at Sweetleaf tastes ever so slightly of honey, and goes down smoothly. Order it straight up or in a macchiato to fully appreciate it.

(347) 527-1038
sweetleafcoffee.com
Subway E, M (Court Sq - 23rd St) or G (21st St - Van Alst)

MON-SUN. 7:00am - 12:00am

First opened 2012
Roaster Sweetleaf Coffee Roasters
Machine La Marzocco GB5, 2 groups
Grinder Mazzer Luigi Robur E, Mahlkönig EK 43

Espresso	$3.00
Cappuccino	$4.00
Latte	$4.50

Sister locations Greenpoint / Jackson Avenue / Queens Plaza

No. 216

Sweetleaf Coffee Roasters

Greenpoint 159 Freeman Street, Brooklyn, NY 11222 | **Greenpoint**

You can't miss Sweetleaf's flagship roastery/cafe, which has the company name stencilled in huge lettering on the exterior. A converted warehouse makes an exceptionally attractive space, wood-beamed and high-ceilinged, and there's plenty of antique seating in both the larger front room and the smaller space in the back, not to mention outside on the benches. Sweetleaf's signature brews are made to a high standard, with lip-smacking cold drinks given equal prominence to the hot stuff.

(347) 987-3732
sweetleafcoffee.com
Subway G (Greenpoint Ave)

Sister locations Queens Plaza /Jackson Avenue / Center Boulevard

MON-FRI. 7:00am - 7:00pm
SAT-SUN. 8:00am - 7:00pm

First opened 2015
Roaster Sweetleaf Coffee Roasters
Machine La Marzocco Strada EP, 2 groups
Grinder Mahlkönig Peak, Mahlkönig EKK 43

Espresso	$3.00
Cappuccino	$4.00
Latte	$4.50

No. 217

Sweetleaf Coffee Roasters

Jackson Avenue 10-93 Jackson Avenue, Queens, NY 11101 | **Long Island City**

The prevailing aesthetic in Long Island City is glass and steel, making the cozy design of Sweetleaf all the more welcome. From couches and a table in the front, you can see through big windows into the bakery where excellent cinnamon donuts and other goodies are made. In the back is a room with a record player where guests are encouraged to pick something out from the collection or bring their records to play. Go for an espresso drink - Sweetleaf roast their own beans nearby.

(917) 832-6726
sweetleafcoffee.com
Subway G (21st St) or 7 (Vernon Blvd - Jackson Ave)

MON-FRI. 7:00am - 7:00pm
SAT-SUN. 8:00am - 7:00pm

First opened 2008
Roaster Sweetleaf Coffee Roasters
Machine La Marzocco Strada EP, 2 groups
Grinder Mazzer Luigi Robur E

Espresso $3.00
Cappuccino $4.00
Latte $4.50

Sister locations Greenpoint / Center Boulevard / Queens Plaza

No. 218

Upright Coffee

860 Manhattan Avenue, Brooklyn, NY 11222 | **Greenpoint**

A gem hidden in Greenpoint, Upright balances seriousness with neighborhood amiability. Using their own Upright blend they pour drinks to impress. The space is streamlined and there are only a few stools, hence the shop's name. Though the compact size of the shop might not give you cause to linger, the care and friendliness of the baristas will. Greenpointers are surely lucky to have it.

uprightcoffee.com
Subway G (Greenpoint Ave)

Sister locations West Village

MON-FRI. 7:00am - 6:00pm
SAT-SUN. 8:00am - 6:00pm

First opened 2011
Roaster Upright Roasting
Machine La Marzocco Linea, 2 groups
Grinder Mazzer Luigi Robur

Espresso $3.50
Cappuccino $4.25
Latte $4.50

No. 219

Variety Coffee Roasters Greenpoint

142 Driggs Avenue, Brooklyn, NY 11222| **Greenpoint**

Since taking on Manhattan, Variety has embraced a renewed focus on smart, luxurious design without compromising the cool, artistic qualities of their Brooklyn roots. Having recently relocated from their original hole-in-the-wall Greenpoint location on Driggs Avenue, the new space across the road is the best of both boroughs. This new, bright, modern corner cafe boasts casual bar seating at a shiny wood counter with gold accents offering prime views of McGolrick Park, real people-watching opportunities, as well as a luxurious brown leather couch in the back, which is apparently too soft for those bearing laptops - score. But as always with Variety, the most successful part of the cafe is the collective of people that work there and the relationships they've built with their producers and the local community.

Third Wave through and through, Variety expertly combines a straightforward, serve-the-people attitude with an enduring commitment to sustainable, single-origin roasts and varied brews. Passionate and dedicated to the craft at every stage, each cup is beautifully prepared, nutty and sweet with any kind of milk, and crisp and clean on its own, always served with smiles and high fives from the counter.

No. 220

MON-SUN. 7:00am - 9:00pm

First opened 2019
Roaster Variety Coffee Roasters
Machine La Marzocco Linea PB ABR, 2 groups
Grinder Mahlkönig E65S

Espresso	$3.00
Cappuccino	$4.00
Latte	$4.50

(718) 282-2326
varietycoffeeroasters.com
Subway G (Nassau Ave)

Sister locations Bushwick / Chelsea / Williamsburg / Upper East Side

The
New York
Coffee
Festival
PROUDLY
OCTOBER 2020
New York's Flagship Coffee Event
@NYCoffeeFest
The New York Coffee Festival
@newyorkcoffeefestival

Photo: Eliza Powell

Behind every cup of coffee is a unique story. On its journey from coffee tree to cup, coffee passes through the hands of a number of skilled individuals. Over the following pages, expert contributors share their specialist knowledge. As you will see, the coffee we enjoy is the result of a rich and complex process, and there is always something new to learn.

Coffee Knowledge

Photo: Horst A. Friedrichs

Coffee at Origin

by **Mike Riley**, Falcon Speciality Green Coffee Importers

If you go into New York's vibrant coffee community today and ask any good barista what makes a perfect cup of coffee, they will always tell you that it starts with the bean. Beyond the roasting technique, the perfect grind, and exact temperatures and precision pressure of a modern espresso machine, we must look to the dedicated coffee farmer who toils away in the tropical lands of Africa, Asia and Latin America. They are the first heroes of our trade.

Approximately 25 million people in over 50 countries are involved in producing coffee. The bean, or seed to be exact, is extracted from cherries that most commonly ripen red but sometimes orange or yellow. The cherries are usually hand-picked then processed by various means. Sometimes they are dried in the fruit under tropical sunshine until they resemble raisins - a process known as 'natural'. The 'honey process' involves pulping the fresh cherries to extract the beans which are then sundried, still coated in their sticky mucilage. Alternatively, in the 'washed process', the freshly pulped beans are left to stand in tanks of water for several hours where enzyme activity breaks down the mucilage, before they are sundried on concrete patios or raised beds. Each method has a profound impact on the ultimate flavor of the coffee.

The term 'speciality coffee' is used to differentiate the world's best from the rest. This means it has to be Arabica, the species of coffee that is often bestowed with incredible flavors - unlike its hardy cousin Robusta which is usually reserved for commercial products and many instant blends. But being Arabica alone is by no means enough for a coffee to achieve the speciality tag, since the best beans are usually those grown at higher altitude on rich and fertile soils. As well as country and region of origin, the variety is important too; Bourbon, Typica, Caturra, Catuai, Pacamara and Geisha to name but a few. Just as Shiraz and Chardonnay grapes have their own complex flavors, the same is true of coffee's varieties. Some of the world's most amazing coffees are the result of the farmer's innovative approach to experimentation with growing and production techniques, meaning that today's speciality roaster is able to source coffees of incredible complexity and variation.

A good coffee establishment will showcase coffees when they are at their best - freshly harvested and seasonal, just like good fruit and vegetables. Seasonal espresso blends change throughout the year to reflect this.

As speciality coffee importers we source stand-out coffees by regularly traveling to origin countries. Direct trade with farmers is always our aim. Above all, we pay sustainable prices and encourage them to treat their land, and those who work it, with respect. Such an approach is increasingly demanded by New York's speciality coffee community in order to safeguard the industry's future.

Photo: Alessandro Bonuzzi

Small Batch Roasting

by **Jonathan Withers**, Green Coffee Buyer, Partners Coffee

Coffee roasted in small batches is a pillar of the specialty coffee industry. It's an essential part of how we elevate our product above the classic American perception of coffee as a simple common commodity. At Partners Coffee, we and our customers celebrate a small batch methodology. It is an artisanal, hand-crafted approach that facilitates and advances deep connections between tradesperson and material, removed from the industrial construct of mass production prioritized above quality; fostering instead a relationship with the client centered on a product made-to-order, carefully and skillfully.

Successfully delivering quality with this approach relies on the implementation of systems which are focused towards consistently achieving a high standard - batch to batch and day to day. From the perspective of the customer, quality is only as high as our ability to fulfill every time. Among the artisanal aspects of small batch roasting, experienced craftspeople have the tools at hand to achieve these high degrees of quality; it's only a matter of applying them towards the goal of consistency.

The operation of small batch equipment allows for the manipulation of multiple controls towards the progress and outcome of a roast: heat via gas burners, airflow via fan speed,damper position, drum speed, and chosen batch size. These variables all independently influence the roast and are essential avenues for exploration in obtaining the sweet-spot. That is the reference profile of how to best roast that coffee in production. Too many variables moving at once however, will diminish the roaster's control over the batch. Once this ideal roasting of a coffee is established, reducing the complexity of variables is key. In most production machines, this is commonly achieved by setting all variables other than gas pressure. Then the batch is controlled solely by manipulating the heat applied to the roaster.

Having limited the variables to simplify and improve repeatability, we need points of feedback with which to monitor and react to controls and results during the roast. Temperature readings at multiple points in the roasting system are essential. These are done with a probe that measures the air exiting the drum and a probe placed awash in the beans to measure the temperature of coffee mass. Gauges on the gas supply and roaster exhaust air allow for hard measurements of the values of heat being applied (burners) and removed (airflow). Associating a reference profile to a static batch size allows these values to serve as a meaningful reference. Therefore, we can replicate the precise conditions and adjustments in future production batches. For recording, collating, and parsing all this data, many options exist to digitally log roasting data and display the information as a referable curve. By drawing the current curve over that of the reference, batches can be skillfully manipulated to be precisely replicated.

After the batch is dropped and cooled, other points to control consistency exist to ensure perfect uniformity. Measuring the weight of the roasted coffee against that of the initial green shows the moisture mass lost during roasting. This number will change as the green coffee ages throughout its lifespan, but from day to day it provides a simple metric as to how similarly the coffee was roasted. More precisely, color analyzers exist which optically meter roasted, ground coffee to give a numeric value indicating the degree to which the coffee has roasted. Cupping your roasted product is of course the most direct connection with the success of the final consistency. Multiple batches appearing together on the same table are incredibly meaningful as they can be directly compared against one another. Carefully recording and collating this sensory data allows a full picture of success as well as areas for focused improvements.

Successfully delivering quality from small batch roasting relies on the skills, talent, and experience of the operator. Yet to ensure that this artistry is maintained and guaranteed with every batch over long days and weeks, a rigorous system of variable control, monitoring metrics and tight quality control is paramount. When they catch problems, you're glad the mistakes weren't able to slip through the cracks.

The Coffee Taster's Flavor Wheel

by **Peter Giuliano**, Chief Research Officer, Specialty Coffee Association

The Coffee Taster's Flavor Wheel has its roots in the World Coffee Research (WCR) Coffee Lexicon project, a piece of scientific research seeking to identify the most common and distinctive flavors that occur in coffee. Over the course of a year, World Coffee Research and the Specialty Coffee Association (SCA) gathered hundreds of samples of coffee, which were analyzed in the Center for Sensory Analysis at Kansas State University. This project identified 110 unique attributes present in coffee and resulted in the publication of the WCR Sensory Lexicon. From there, SCA went to the Food Science and Technology department of UC Davis, where researchers designed a unique, sophisticated sensory research project to understand how tasters organized taste attributes, leading to the design of the SCA/WCR Coffee Taster's Flavor Wheel.

In all, the Coffee Taster's Flavor Wheel is the product of the largest collaborative coffee sensory science research project in history and reflects the work of dozens of coffee tasters and sensory scientists over hundreds of hours. The Coffee Taster's Flavor Wheel is used by coffee professionals every day to help evaluate and describe coffee's tastes, flavors and aromas. The wheel has been translated into 10 languages and is seen in tasting rooms and sensory laboratories all over the world.

How to use the wheel

Though the Coffee Taster's Flavor Wheel is based in rigorous research and sensory science, it is easy for even a novice to use. The flavors (called 'attributes') are arranged on the wheel according to how coffee tasters actually use them making the use of the wheel very intuitive. The trick is to begin at the center: after tasting a coffee, simply begin by identifying a flavor in one of the 9 'first tier' attributes in the innermost level of the wheel.
Say you choose 'fruity'. From there, the taster choses one of the 4 'second tier' attributes. Say you choose 'citrus fruit'. From there, you can choose among four specific citrus fruits. In this way, the taster moves from general to specific tastes, helping zero in on specific attributes in a methodical but simple way.

The Coffee Taster's Flavor Wheel© encourages coffee lovers of all kinds to enjoy and make use of this valuable tool. To learn more, visit **www.sca.coffee**.

SCA

Coffee Taster's Flavor Wheel

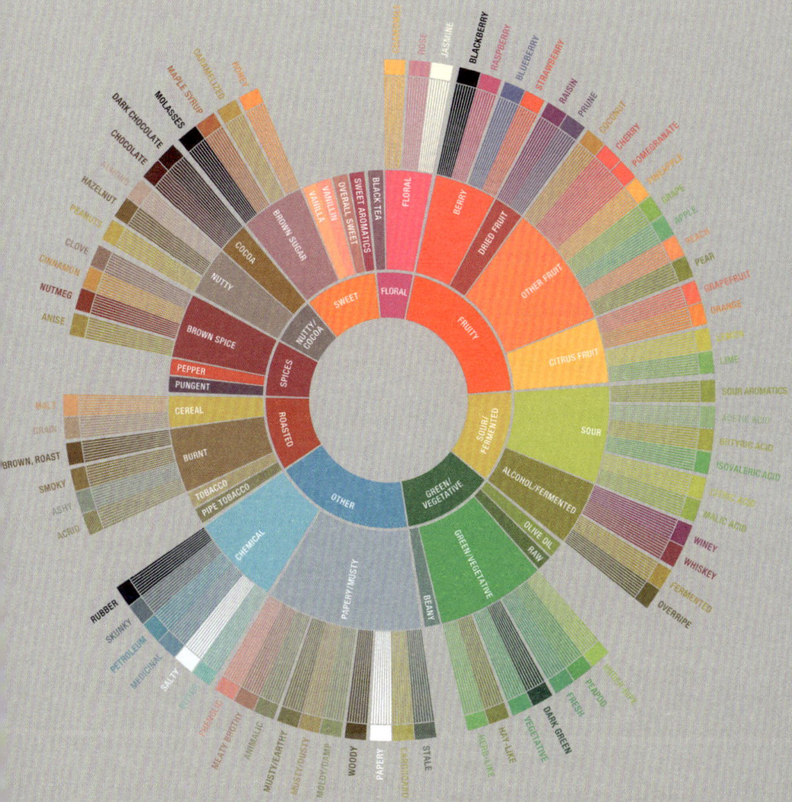

FLORAL: BLACK TEA; FLORAL (CHAMOMILE, ROSE, JASMINE)

FRUITY: BERRY (BLACKBERRY, RASPBERRY, BLUEBERRY, STRAWBERRY); DRIED FRUIT (RAISIN, PRUNE); OTHER FRUIT (COCONUT, CHERRY, POMEGRANATE, PINEAPPLE, GRAPE, APPLE, PEACH, PEAR); CITRUS FRUIT (GRAPEFRUIT, ORANGE, LEMON, LIME)

SOUR/FERMENTED: SOUR (SOUR AROMATICS, ACETIC ACID, BUTYRIC ACID, ISOVALERIC ACID, CITRIC ACID, MALIC ACID); ALCOHOL/FERMENTED (WINEY, WHISKEY, FERMENTED, OVERRIPE)

GREEN/VEGETATIVE: OLIVE OIL; RAW; GREEN/VEGETATIVE (UNDER-RIPE, PEAPOD, FRESH, DARK GREEN, VEGETATIVE, HAY-LIKE, HERB-LIKE); BEANY

OTHER: PAPERY/MUSTY (STALE, CARDBOARD, PAPERY, WOODY, MOLDY/DAMP, MUSTY/DUSTY, MUSTY/EARTHY, ANIMALIC, MEATY BROTHY, PHENOLIC); CHEMICAL (BITTER, SALTY, MEDICINAL, PETROLEUM, SKUNKY, RUBBER)

ROASTED: PIPE TOBACCO; TOBACCO; BURNT (ACRID, ASHY, SMOKY, BROWN, ROAST); CEREAL (GRAIN, MALT)

SPICES: PUNGENT; PEPPER; BROWN SPICE (ANISE, NUTMEG, CINNAMON, CLOVE)

NUTTY/COCOA: NUTTY (PEANUTS, HAZELNUT, ALMOND); COCOA (CHOCOLATE, DARK CHOCOLATE)

SWEET: BROWN SUGAR (MOLASSES, MAPLE SYRUP, CARAMELIZED, HONEY); VANILLA; VANILLIN; OVERALL SWEET; SWEET AROMATICS

COFFEE TASTER'S FLAVOR WHEEL CREATED USING THE SENSORY LEXICON DEVELOPED BY WORLD COFFEE RESEARCH

V.2

Coffee Grinding

by **Jeremy Challender**, Former Co-owner and Director of Training, Prufrock Coffee and the

Grinder technology is about to change radically. Machine design, techniques behind the bar and hand brewing methodology have improved rapidly over recent years. Manufacturers are starting to address this by seeking feedback from users as well as lab testing. Home users can benefit from these changes too. New designs entering the market have drawn directly from the experiences of barista champions. Grinder designers are seeking professional and consumer feedback on taste, flavor and ergonomics through direct collaboration and field testing. Manufacturers are aware that we need development to continue and, now more than ever, baristas have a voice in this process. To be a barista in this time of grinder development is very exciting.

With all brew methods the challenge is replicating flavor and strength. Once we've got a precise brew recipe for a coffee we stand a better chance of extracting our coffee consistently. Commercially, the easiest way to navigate from this baseline towards the optimum extraction level is with micro-adjustments in the exposed surface area of the grinds - so the grinder is key to managing flavor in the cup.

The challenge grinder designers face is how to create consistency of grind size and shape. If you get out the microscope, and a set of test sieves, you start to realize all your grinds aren't the same size, nor are they all the same shape. If they were all the same size and shape, brewing would be much easier to control. In espresso you will have seen tiny granules in your cup that are smaller than the holes in the filter basket. We call these fines. These small particles have very high surface area and extract very quickly. As a home brewer, you could consider following the example of many championship baristas; invest in laboratory test sieves to remove a portion of particles under a certain size to reduce over-extracted flavors.

There is a portion of particles that fit side-on between the burrs and are planed rather than ground. We call these larger particles boulders. They have a much lower surface area relative to their size and in a 30 second espresso extraction will under-extract. Wobbly hand grinders are real offenders in the production of boulders. These too can be sieved out.

Sharp burrs are considered to reduce fines production. Ceramic burrs, which many hand grinders are fitted with, are very durable but are often not very sharp to start with. The material of choice at the moment is titanium-coated steel. Large burr diameter is linked to lower production of fines and boulders (more 'modal' distribution) so enormous bag grinders are being examined for application in espresso making. Cutting systems like spice grinders produce a very high proportion of fines and boulders, so are not recommended.

Keeping the coffee cool during grinding is a challenge. Burrs get hot in use because of friction, and some of the most exciting developments recently have focused on temperature stability of the burrs and burr casing with the addition of heating elements and fans. A warm grinder behaves differently to a cold or a hot one, so the particle shape and size are dependent on both grind setting and temperature.

Modern grinder design is very focused on ease of access for regular cleaning. Arabica coffee has up to 17% fat content. We only extract a small percentage of this into a beverage but even after a day of commercial use, a grinder will have a slick of fats and tiny fine particles built up around the burr casing and the barrel and throat of the grinder. Oils oxidise, so grinders must be opened up and thoroughly swept out on a regular basis. Burrs can be washed in soapy water or coffee cleaner, or abrasive oil absorbing grinder cleaning granules can be used. Home baristas have an advantage here by being able to clean after a few shots rather than after a full day's usage.

The final hurdle to overcome is grind retention: many grinders on the market have large barrels and throats that can store as much as 40g of grinds that must be squeezed out before fresh grinds appear. At Prufrock, we are moving away from grinders with a high retention of grinds as we are looking to optimize freshness. When grind changes are required we want the benefit of micro-adjustment to be immediate. Here, home baristas are also well placed, as hand grinders have zero retention of grinds and some very high quality espresso hand grinders are now available on the market.

Over the last decade we have felt that machine technology has been in advance of grinders. We often comment that a barista's top priority should be the choice of grinder. Find a great grinding solution and great coffee will follow.

Photo: Jacob Thue

Water - The Enigma

by **Maxwell Colonna-Dashwood**, Co-owner, Colonna and Small's, UK Barista Champion 2012 & 2014

This vital ingredient is the foundation of every cup of coffee you have ever tasted, apart from the bean itself of course.

It's not just coffee that relies so dramatically on this everyday and seemingly straightforward substance. The worlds of craft beer and whiskey are suitable comparisons, with breweries and distilleries proudly signifying the provenance of their water as being a vital part of their product.

A roaster, though, sells coffee, the water bit comes post sale. The water will be different and unique based on the locality of brewing, and this is on top of all of the other variables that define coffee brewing such as grinding, temperature and brew ratios. The reality is that the impact of water is rarely directly witnessed, with the other variables often being seen as the cause for dramatic flavor changes. You may be wondering right now, how big an impact can it really have?

I'm yet to present the same coffee brewed with different waters to drinkers and not have them exclaim 'I can't believe how different they are, they taste like different coffees'. These aren't 'coffee people' either, but customers who contested prior to the tasting that 'you may be able to taste the difference but I doubt I can tell.'

It may make you question whether the coffee that you tried and weren't particularly keen on, was a representative version of what the bean actually tastes like, or at the least what it is capable of tasting of like.

So, why the big difference, what is in the water?

Nearly all water that trickles out of a tap or sits in a bottle is not just water. As well as the H2O there are other bits and bobs in the water. Minerals mainly. These have a big impact not only on what we extract from the coffee but also how that flavor sits in the cup of coffee.

It's fair to say that currently the way the coffee industry discusses water is through the use of a measurement called Total Dissolved Solids (TDS).

TDS has become the measurement which is relied upon to distinguish and inform us about how water will affect our coffee. It gives us a total of everything in the water. The problem though, is that TDS doesn't tell us everything we need to know about the water; it doesn't tell us about what those solids are. On top of this, TDS meters don't measure some non-solids that have a huge impact on flavor.

In the water, we need the minerals calcium and magnesium to help pull out a lot of the desirable flavor in the coffee, but we also need the right amount of buffering ability in the water to balance the acids. This buffering ability can be noted as the

bicarbonate content of the water.
So for example an 'empty' soft water with no minerals will lack flavor complexity and the lack of buffer will mean a more vinegary acidity.

However the coffee shops in this guide will most likely have a trick up their sleeve. The industry filtration systems that have been developed primarily to stop scale build up in the striking and valuable espresso machines, also produce water compositions that are more often than not preferable for coffee brewing. Speciality coffee shops require all manner of specifics to be obsessed over and carefully executed. That cup of coffee that hits you and stops you in your step with intense, balanced and complex flavor will owe its brilliance to careful brewing, a knowledgeable brewer and superb equipment. However, it also owes a significant part of its beautiful character and flavor to the water it is brewed with.

Photo: Samuel Scrimshaw

Espresso

by **Bill McAllister**, Director of the Service Department, Irving Farm New York

The definition of espresso is a method of brewing coffee according to the Specialty Coffee Association of America, a trade group that represents and undoubtedly has some direct connection to every person and place in this book. Yet the difference between a coffee made using a Chemex versus a vacuum pot or any other coffee maker is negligible compared to what an espresso machine produces. The root cause is pressure. Espresso machines take water that would normally be poured or sprinkled onto coffee and forces it through the pressure of the atmosphere. But who came up with that? How did they know it could make coffee so much more delicious than normal?

The etymology of espresso reveals a lot about the intention of this technology. If we Anglicize the word into 'expresso', it is easy to see that the drink needs to be made quickly, but also that it needs to be made expressly for a consumer. Back in Italian, it's just as easily interpreted as 'to press out', bringing pressure back into the picture. Put it all together, and you have a device that makes coffee quickly, one at a time, using pressure. All of this is according to Andrea Illy (yes, that Illy) as written in Espresso Coffee, one of the few textbooks on coffee.

It paints a somewhat primitive picture of Italy in the 1880s, where the first patents for espresso machines are traced. The technology at the time was coarse and rugged. It relied on huge boilers heated by fire that used a head of steam to push water through the ground coffee. A barista would be hard-pressed to make anything that wasn't quite bitter. This was espresso for decades. But then, manufacturers introduced a lever and piston as an alternative method of generating pressure. This change allowed the machines to be much smaller, brew at pressures that have become today's standard, and use water that isn't super-heated. All of a sudden espresso carts became a reality, bringing the means of caffeination to even more people. But the most important part of the change in the machines is that it is no longer impossible for a shot to be pulled that is more than something used as a dose of energy.

The espresso of today and its potential to be mind-blowingly delicious has a culture surrounding it that elevates it above the rest of coffee. Cafes have moved far beyond just dishing out shots to give workers a boost mid-afternoon. A coffee shop that wants to be the talk of the town these days draws customers in by talking about the specific farms their coffee is from, the agronomy of the plant from which the coffee is harvested, and a level of precision that requires scales that wouldn't be out of place in a display on St Marks Place.

How we went from pre-industrial caffeine machines relying on levers and pistons to today's models doesn't contain any big eureka moments, but is mostly a steady stream of smart revisions. Baristas realized early on that their ability to reliably make the most delicious espresso they've tasted required having a machine they could count on to work the same way every time. To this end, springs and levers were replaced by electric pumps and gas burners were replaced by heating elements controlled by computers. Yet with all of these, advances were driven by the trial and error of passionate baristas, because despite the long history of espresso, there is not a lot of scientific writing about the process with which it is made. When a handful of videos featuring clear plastic portafilters started trickling out in the last few years, coffee pros everywhere were astounded - the first real evidence in over a century as to what's happening when making espresso!

Explanations of how and why espresso works may be lacking, but we can still gather a few lessons as consumers. A properly prepared shot looks elegant as it pours into a cup, flowing thick but steady, like warm honey, a promise of flavor that delivers on the intoxicating smell characteristic of coffee shops everywhere. At its best, a coffee brewed as espresso sees its flavors held under a magnifying glass. The experience is intense, but often divisive: fruity Ethiopian coffees taste like someone plopped jam in the bottom of your demitasse, so lush with fruit flavor and sweetness it seems impossible that the only ingredient is coffee. The second you sip a good espresso, all thoughts of history are fleeting memories; your thoughts are now on the delicious beverage in your hands.

Brewing Coffee at Home

by **Christian Baker, David Robson, Sam Mason & The New York Coffee Guide**

You may be surprised to know that coffee brewed at home can rival that of your favorite coffee shop. All you need is good quality ingredients and some inexpensive equipment. Keep in mind that small variations in grind coarseness, coffee/water ratio and brew time will make a significant difference to flavor, and that trial and error is the key to unlocking perfection.

Whole Beans: Whole bean coffee is superior to pre-ground. Coffee rapidly deteriorates once ground, so buy your coffee in whole bean form and store it in an air-tight container at room temperature. It should be consumed between three and thirty days after roast and ground only moments before brewing.

Water: We often forget that water makes up over 98% of the finished drink. Use filtered or bottled water, preferably with a dry residue between 80-150mg/l. Most regular tap water will inhibit your ability to extract flavor and reveal only a fraction of a coffee's potential.

Digital scales: Get a set of scales accurate to 1g and large enough to hold your coffee brewer. Coffee is commonly measured in 'scoops' or 'tablespoons', but coffee and water are best measured by weight for greater accuracy and to ensure repeatability. Small changes in the ratio of coffee to water can have a significant impact on flavor. A good starting point is 60-70g of coffee per litre of water. Apply this ratio to meet the size of your brewer.

Grinder

A burr grinder is essential. Burr grinders are superior to blade grinders because they allow the grind coarseness to be set and produce a more consistent size of coffee fragment (critical for an even extraction). As a general rule, the coarser the grind the longer the brew time required, and vice versa. For example, an espresso needs a very fine grind whereas a French Press works with a coarser grind.

French Press

Preheat the French Press with hot water, and discard. Add 34g of coarsely ground coffee and pour in 500g of water just below boiling point (201-203°F). Steep for 4 to 5 minutes then gently plunge to the bottom. Decant the coffee straight away to avoid over-brewing (known as over-extraction).

AeroPress

The AeroPress is wonderfully versatile. It can be used with finely ground coffee and a short steep time, or with a coarser grind and a longer steep time. The latter is our preferred method for its flavor and repeatability. Preheat the AeroPress using hot water, and discard. Rinse the paper filter before securing, and place the AeroPress over a sturdy cup or jug. Add 16g of coffee and pour in 240g of water at 203°F. Secure the plunger on top, creating a seal. Steep for 3 minutes then plunge over 20 seconds.

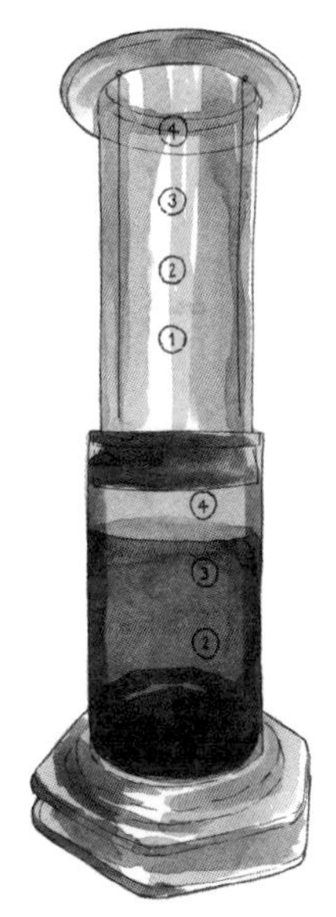

Pour Over

We recommend using a pouring kettle for better pouring control. Place a filter paper in the cone and rinse through with hot water. Add 15g of coffee and slowly pour 30g of 203°F water to pre-soak the coffee grounds. This creates the 'bloom'. After 30 seconds add 250g of water, pouring steadily in a circular motion over the center. It should take 1 minute and 45 seconds to pour and between 30-45 seconds to drain through. The key is to keep the flow of water steady. If the water drains too quickly/slowly, adjust the coarseness of the grind to compensate.

Stovetop

A stovetop will not make an espresso, it will, however, make a strong coffee. Pour hot water into the base to the fill-line or just below the pressure release valve. Fill the basket with ground coffee of medium coarseness (between Pour Over and French Press). Traditional wisdom suggests a fine grind in pursuit of espresso, but stovetops extract differently to espresso machines and grinding fine is a recipe for bitter, over-extracted coffee. Screw the base to the top and place on the heat. When you hear bubbling, remove immediately and decant to ensure the brewing has stopped.

Illustrations: Zoë Barker

Traditional Pump Espresso Machine

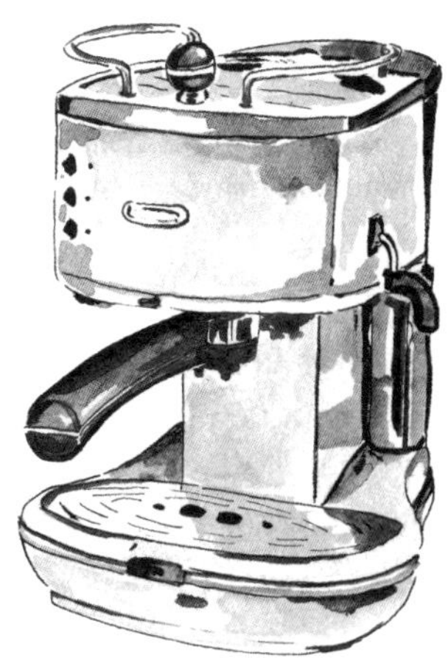

Traditional pump espresso machines are ideal for that barista experience to create espresso-based coffee at home. Coffee should be freshly and finely ground and dosed into single or double shot filter baskets. It is then tamped to extract full flavor aroma and coffee crema. The machine controls temperature for a more consistent cup. To enjoy milk drinks such as flat whites and cappuccinos simply froth fresh milk using the steam wand (stay below 158°F) and top up your espresso.

Bean to Cup Machine

Bean to Cup provides the perfect 'coffee shop' fix and fast. It gives you all the versatility of choice and personalization of a traditional pump machine. At the touch of a button, it burr-grinds fresh beans and froths milk (some machines even have a built in carafe), creating a fresh taste for your cup. You can personalize the strength, length, temperature, and even the froth setting. One-touch drink options make your personalized coffee time and again, without mess or fuss.

Illustrations: Sara Gelfgren

Latte Art

by **Jai Lott**, Coffee Director for Bluestone Lane

Latte art is the barista's signature in a milk based espresso drink.

Over the years latte art has shifted from being 'etched' chocolate sauce designs and foamy 'hand spooned' structures, to a fragile and carefully constructed pattern where the slightest movement of the hand can make or break a masterpiece.

There are 3 major components to world-class latte art: espresso, milk and execution.

1 Espresso

Perfect espresso is your canvas. Well-executed fresh extraction with a thick stable crema sets the foundation for your latte art. A double shot or around 40 grams of yield and medium roast is a great starting point. This helps create contrast in the cup. Espresso and milk preparation should happen simultaneously to ensure crema does not have time to dissipate.

2 Milk

The colder your milk, the better. This gives it more chances at rotation in the pitcher before reaching temperature, which in turn increases your milk's texture. Once the steam wand is in position slightly below the surface of the milk and sits slightly off center, engage the wand and slowly lower the jug adding small amounts of air while simultaneously keeping the milk spinning solid. All air should be added prior to the milk reaching room temperature for great results. Turn off the steam when you reach your desired temperature.

Ideal learning tools:

- A steaming pitcher that has perfect spout symmetry. Using the same jug every time is vital to getting comfortable with latte art.
- A wide ceramic cup of around 8oz is great to start with. This gives you plenty of breathing space.
- An environment where you can concentrate and not be bumped!

3 Execution

If everything worked out (and trust me it takes practice even getting to this point) you should have beautiful espresso and a hot pitcher with milk resembling freshly applied paint. Its time to pour!

Tilting the cup at 45 degrees, pour into the center of the espresso at a height of 2-3 inches. Imagine a diving board and a diver trying to pierce the espresso without disrupting the surface. Keep an even flow for the entire pour.

Once the liquid gets to the low edge of the cup, two things need to happen:

Firstly, flatten out the cup while simultaneously bringing the pitcher all the way down to almost full contact with the espresso. This will increase the amount of microfoam allowed from behind the pitchers spout and a white dot will begin to appear (remember keep the same flow the whole time!).

Secondly, in the final moment of the pour, exit the cup by lifting the jug and cutting through the center of your white dot. Imagine the milk from the spout is an airplane taking off.

Perfect love heart!

Once you master our love hearts, move on to a two-stack tulip.

The big secret - stick to one design for days, weeks if needed. Get each design mastered before progressing to the next. This is the way to get good fast and an understanding of what each movement will result in.

Spill milk, make a mess and most importantly have fun! That's what coffee should be all about. Just don't forget that latte art certainly makes coffee look great, but great espresso and milk are more important!

What Does 'Local' Coffee Mean?

by **Teresa von Fuchs**, Sales Director at Volcafe Specialty

When the Eastman Egg Company in Chicago revamped their coffee program, they didn't partner with a company from Chicago. Even though there are great roasters in the area, they found that the partnership that met all of their goals and matched their values was New York. This got them thinking about ways to quickly explain this choice to their customers and what 'local' means in coffee.

Local coffee isn't as straightforward as local eggs, local arugula or even local bread (which may or may not contain locally grown and milled grain!). By necessity, coffee must travel hundreds and thousands of miles. Most people who drink coffee every day in the U.S. have never seen a coffee tree in person - they might not even know that coffee starts as a fruit. Given the distance from the source, it's challenging for most people to truly grasp the vast amount of work that must happen before coffee ends up in your cup. Yet it's this connection and understanding to where something comes from and how it's made that people seek when they look for 'local' products.

In the journal 'Renewable Agriculture and Food Systems' CJ Peters writes, 'Most researchers accept that eating locally means minimizing the distance between production and consumption'. When the Food Marketing Institute conducted a study asking Americans across the country why they buy local, knowing where a product came from was in the top three responses. Supporting the local economy came in second. While it's logistically not possible to actually shorten the distance between where coffee is grown and all the places it's consumed, there are ways to bring producers and consumers closer together. For coffee, 'local' is about relationships and knowledge, not 'locale.'

For the team at Eastman, it was the connection their new roasting partner helped forge with the farms and people growing and processing their coffee that helped them answer the questions about why their roaster wasn't 'local.' It wasn't about where the roastery was located. It was about developing a connection to the process from seed to cup that made their coffee more local.

What I love about this lens is that it can extend everyone's experience of coffee, not just cafe owners looking for a roaster. When you go to your local cafe, the staff know you. They remember what you drink, your name, what days or times you usually come in, snippets of conversations you've shared. It's your cafe. And that cafe is your opportunity for local coffee. Whether you want to know the exact altitude of the farm where the coffee was grown or not, you can still participate in minimizing the distance between the production of coffee and drinking it. Get to know your barista. What do they drink? Why do they work there? What do they like about coffee?

If you buy beans from a store to brew at home, find out about the roaster. Where do they get the beans from? How did they start roasting coffee? What do they love about it?

The longer I work in coffee, the more expanded my idea of 'local' and 'community' becomes. When I taste coffee, I think about the places and the people that grow the coffee, all the hands that pick and process and pack and ship that coffee. I think about how far it travels to where it will be roasted. I think about who roasted it. When I go to a cafe for coffee, I think about all that, as well as the care and time someone took to craft it into a cup. When I sip, I feel connected to that whole world.

Education & Training

by **Allie Caran**, Director of Education, Partners Coffee

One of the greatest achievements in the advancement of Specialty Coffee has been its impressive growth of coffee education. In the past decade we have witnessed the research, development and implementation of standardized coffee education on a world-wide level. Organizations such as the Specialty Coffee Association (SCA) have spearheaded the conversation by representing individuals throughout the coffee supply chain, creating a cohesive shared experience and an impressive global network.

For those looking to learn more about coffee, or ultimately to create a greater depth of knowledge, the SCA offers pathways like the New Coffee Skills Program. These programs offer both industry professionals and consumers a way to explore various aspects of coffee; brewing, sensory skills, and even roasting. With education being at the forefront of coffee, many roasteries have created similar models of educational classes and certifications.

When Partners Coffee (named Toby's Estate at the time) opened in 2012, there was a recognized lack of educational resources for coffee professionals and consumers alike. We built two state-of-the-art Coffee Labs and selected the industry's best coffee leaders to educate both baristas and coffee lovers.

Our Coffee Educators continually foster a culture of curiosity and knowledge, providing a thoughtful and focused forum for learning that includes hands-on practice as well as theory. Similar to the New Coffee Skills Program, students can choose to hone-in and learn more about any specific topic in the world of coffee in a private class setting; brewing, sustainability, green buying, and sensory analysis. Additionally, we offer an in-house Certification Program for baristas. Upon completion of all modules, baristas are tested in both written and practical formats to assess written comprehension and technical expertise in coffee, giving them the tools they need to be exceptional Coffee Professionals.

Our program, like many, revolves around the advancement of knowledge in coffee. It is an experience open to anyone and everyone. As the industry continues to evolve, education and shared knowledge will be the keystone to successful growth.

Photo: Partners Coffee

Coffee History in New York City

by **Erin Meister**, Coffee Professional, Journalist & Author of a forthcoming book about NYC's coff

What makes New York a coffee town, exactly? Is it the reputation as the 'city that never sleeps,' or the fact that caffeine is necessary to get anything done in a New York minute? Do residents of the city drink an estimated 25 percent more coffee than anyone else in the country because the stuff can be bought on every street corner? Or could it be the other way around - that the sheer ubiquity of the stuff is what makes it practically a way of life for locals? Does it mean something that the average cup costs less than a copy of the daily paper?

No matter the reason, facts are facts: New York and coffee are made for each other.

Of course it's true that the regular Joes here simply love their 'regular' joe (which usually means a cup of drip with milk and sugar, in deli shorthand). But there's actually more coffee flowing in the veins of the city than even gets poured on its surface. So much of what happens with coffee here is behind-the-scenes that most New Yorkers don't even know quite how caffeinated they really are. Even the history of the city and the beverage go all the way back - further, actually, than the name 'New York.' The coffee habit actually got brewed up when the city was still New Amsterdam, under Dutch control.

From the green-coffee contracts to the containers they come in, to the roasting machines that turn them from hard little seeds into semi-precious brown beans, New York has had a tremendous influence on every step in the journey of billions of bags, brews, and cups.

The city's position as an East Coast hub has allowed for its unique junction of caffeine and culture, not only just among its fellow American metro centers, but also worldwide. The coffee history here has influenced global market structures, supply and demand trends, shipping routes and intercontinental trade, roasting and preparation technology and innovation, marketing strategy, and even cafe life. The first truly successful commercial coffee-roasting machine was patented by a New Yorker, Jabez Burns, whose company would go on to become one of the most enduring and consistently innovative in the industry for over 130 years. The Green Coffee Association of New York was founded as the first significant overseeing body to ensure, and insure, the integrity and fulfillment of contracts. Depending on whom you ask, the first espresso machine in the country was imported and installed either uptown at Barbetta Restaurant in 1911 or downtown at Caffè Reggio, which opened in 1927.

The combination of a crush of people from all types and all walks, overwhelming sparking creative energy, and the fearlessness of failure is certainly in part to thank, but coffee itself contributes something to the dynamic and living nature of New York - it keeps the gears turning.

There is also a special something about New York City that not just allows for rebirth and reinvention, but actually thrives on it. Perhaps the most classic 'only in New York' moments in the timeline of coffee's history here is the fact that one of the very men who was responsible for the first tremendous 'coffee collapse' in 1880 - a failed attempted corner on the coffee market by a syndicate of large brokerage houses, the result of which was widespread bankruptcy and at least one alleged coffee suicide - was elected just two years later to serve as the first president of the Coffee Exchange, which his misadventure had inspired the coffee men to create.

That's only one of hundreds of 'only in New York' stories, of course. Here's another in 1907, a woman named Alice Foote MacDougall used her last $38 to establish herself as the only female coffee broker in the waterfront Coffee District. Within two decades she was signing a $1 million lease on her fifth hugely successful coffee shop - the modern equivalent of nearly $14 million. Just like the city itself, MacDougall was a beautiful mess of contradictions. Though she was a successful business owner herself, she regularly advised women to stay at home and out of the commercial and corporate worlds, and was an ardent anti-suffragist.

From coffeehouse counter-culture in the late 1950s and 1960s, to the Central Perk-inspired, overstuffed, mismatched cafe of the 90s, to the minimal and coffee-quality-obsessed espresso and slow-pour bars of the early 2000s; NYC coffee shops have always managed to define their era. They have been capturing and capitalizing on the shifting moods and cravings of 8 million people, even if only for a finite period. The coffee lovers of today in Brooklyn, Manhattan, and Queens (the Bronx and Staten Island will catch up eventually) go about their daily rituals, drinking their morning cups or evening espresso, knowing full well that there's no telling what will be on the next generation of menus, in the next wave of shops.

Beyond the bars, there are the beans. Millions and millions of bags of them that travel through New York every year, on their way to roasters and consumers around the country and world. Despite the fact that New Jersey actually claims the country's first fully containerized shipping port, this transformed the intercontinental transit of loads of green coffee and knocked a few pegs out of NYC's dominance in that arena.

Even the world's most famous mermaid has a Brooklyn connection: Starbucks' former chairman and CEO Howard Schultz grew up in the Canarsie section of the borough - a neighborhood that perhaps ironically remains a good-coffee desert today, but even that will surely change with time.

Gotham's inexhaustible need to create, destroy, and re-create might make it difficult to keep up with the trends (or 'waves,' if we must). But at least we can all be assured that the revolutions will be caffeinated. 'There is something in the New York air that makes sleep useless,' wrote Simone de Beauvoir in 1947, and it's as true today as it was then, only the answer is obvious. It must simply be the coffee.

Coffee Glossary

Acidity: the pleasant tartness of a coffee. Examples of acidity descriptors include lively and flat. One of the principal attributes evaluated by professional tasters when determining the quality of a coffee.

AeroPress: a hand-powered coffee brewer marketed by Aerobie Inc., and launched in 2005. Consists of two cylinders, one sliding within the other, somewhat resembling a large syringe. Water is forced through ground coffee held in place by a paper filter, creating a concentrated filter brew.

Affogato: one or more scoops of vanilla ice cream topped with a shot of espresso, served as a dessert.

Americano, Caffè Americano: a long coffee consisting of espresso with hot water added on top. Originates from the style of coffee favored by American GIs stationed in Europe during WWII.

Arabica, Coffea arabica: the earliest cultivated species of coffee tree and the most widely grown, Arabica accounts for approximately 70% of the world's coffee. Superior in quality to Robusta, it is more delicate and is generally grown at higher altitudes.

Aroma: the fragrance produced by brewed coffee. Examples of aroma descriptors include earthy, spicy and floral. One of the principal attributes evaluated by professional tasters when determining the quality of a coffee.

Barista: a professional person skilled in making coffee, particularly one working at an espresso bar.

Blend: a combination of coffees from different countries or regions. Mixed together, they achieve a balanced flavor profile no single coffee can offer alone.

Body: describes the heaviness, thickness or relative weight of coffee on the tongue. One of the principal attributes evaluated by professional tasters when determining the quality of a coffee.

Bottomless portafilter, naked portafilter: a portafilter without spouts, allowing espresso to flow directly from the bottom of the filter basket into the cup. Allows the extraction to be monitored visually.

Brew group: the assembly protruding from the front of an espresso machine consisting of the grouphead, portafilter and basket. The brew group must be heated to a sufficient temperature to produce a good espresso.

Brew pressure: pressure of 9 bar is required for espresso extraction.

Brew temperature: the water temperature at the point of contact with coffee. Optimum brew temperature varies by extraction method. Espresso brew temperature is typically 194-203°F. A stable brew temperature is crucial for good espresso.

Brew time, extraction time: the contact time between water and coffee. Espresso brew time is typically 25-30 seconds. Brew times are dictated by a variety of factors including the grind coarseness and degree of roast.

Burr set: an integral part of a coffee grinder. Consists of a pair of rotating steel discs between which coffee beans are ground. Burrs are either flat or conical in shape.

Café con leche: a traditional Spanish coffee consisting of espresso topped with scalded milk.

Caffeine: an odorless, slightly bitter alkaloid responsible for the stimulating effect of coffee.

Cappuccino: a classic Italian coffee comprising espresso, steamed milk and topped with a layer of foam. Traditionally served in a 6oz cup and sometimes topped with powdered chocolate or cinnamon.

Capsule: a self-contained, pre-ground, pre-pressed portion of coffee, individually sealed inside a plastic capsule. Capsule brewing systems are commonly found in domestic coffee machines. Often compatible only with certain equipment brands.

Chemex: A type of pour over coffee brewer with a distinctive hourglass-shaped vessel. Invented in 1941, the Chemex has become regarded as a design classic and is on permanent display at the Museum of Modern Art in New York City.

Cherry: the fruit of the coffee plant. Each cherry contains two coffee seeds (beans).

Cold brew: Cold brew refers to the process of steeping coffee grounds in room temperature or cold water for an extended period. Cold brew coffee is not to be confused with iced coffee.

Cortado: a traditional short Spanish coffee consisting of espresso cut with a small quantity of steamed milk. Similar to an Italian piccolo.

Crema: the dense caramel-colored layer that forms on the surface of an espresso. Consists of emulsified oils created by the dispersion of gases in liquid at high pressure. The presence of crema is commonly equated with a good espresso.

Cupping: a method by which professional tasters perform sensory evaluation of coffee. Hot water is poured over ground coffee and left to extract. The taster first samples the aroma, then tastes the coffee by slurping it from a spoon.

Decaffeinated: coffee with approximately 97% or more of its naturally occurring caffeine removed is classified as decaffeinated.

Dispersion screen, shower screen: a component of the grouphead that ensures even distribution of brewing water over the coffee bed in the filter basket.

Dosage: the mass of ground coffee used for a given brewing method. Espresso dosage is typically 7-10g of ground coffee (14-20g for a double).

Double espresso, doppio: typically 30-50ml extracted from 14-20g of ground coffee. The majority of coffee venues in this guide serve double shots as standard.

Drip method: a brewing method that allows brew water to seep through a bed of ground coffee by gravity, not pressure.

Espresso: the short, strong shot of coffee that forms the basis for many other coffee beverages. Made by forcing hot water at high pressure through a compressed bed of finely ground coffee.

Espresso machine: in a typical configuration, a pump delivers hot water from a boiler to the brew group, where it is forced under pressure through ground coffee held in the portafilter. A separate boiler delivers steam for milk steaming.

Extraction: the process of infusing coffee with hot water to release flavor, accomplished either by allowing ground coffee to sit in hot water for a period of time or by forcing hot water through ground coffee under pressure.

Fifth Wave / 5th Wave™: A new era for the coffee industry signifying the creation of 'boutique at scale'. This means aspiring to and achieving the highest quality of output across one's business or cafe, including, but not limited to, atmosphere, coffee quality, service level, staff training, business and IT systems. This era represents an advance on previous 'waves' most notably the 3rd Wave or artisan coffee era typified by craft coffee, or The 4th Wave, the science of coffee. 5th Wave businesses tend to be aspirational, professionally run businesses targeting a savvy millennial audience.

Filter method: any brewing method in which water filters through a bed of ground coffee. Most commonly used to describe drip method brewers that use a paper filter to separate grounds from brewed coffee.

Flat white: an espresso-based beverage first made popular in Australia and New Zealand. Made with a double shot of espresso with finely steamed milk and a thin layer of microfoam. Typically served as a 5-6oz drink with latte art.

Flavor: the way a coffee tastes. Flavor descriptors include nutty and earthy. One of the principal attributes evaluated by professional tasters when determining the quality of a coffee.

French press, plunger pot, cafetiere: a brewing method that separates grounds from brewed coffee by pressing them to the bottom of the brewing receptacle with a mesh filter attached to a plunger.

Green coffee, green beans: unroasted coffee. The dried seeds from the coffee cherry.

Grind: the degree of coarseness to which coffee beans are ground. A crucial factor in determining the nature of a coffee brew. Grind coarseness should be varied in accordance with the brewing method. Methods involving longer brew times call for a coarse grind. A fine grind is required for brew methods with a short extraction time such as espresso.

Grinder: a vital piece of equipment for making coffee. Coffee beans must be ground evenly for a good extraction. Most commonly motorised, but occasionally manual. Burr grinders are the best choice for an even grind.

Group: see Brew Group

Grouphead: a component of the brew group containing the locking connector for the portafilter and the dispersion screen.

Honey process, pulped natural, semi-washed: a method of processing coffee where the cherry is removed (pulped), but the beans are sun-dried with mucilage intact. Typically results in a sweet flavor profile with a balanced acidity.

Latte, caffè latte: an Italian beverage made with espresso combined with steamed milk, traditionally topped with foamed milk and served in a glass. Typically at least 8oz in volume, usually larger.

Latte art: the pattern or design created by pouring steamed milk on top of espresso. Only finely steamed milk is suitable for creating latte art. Popular patterns include the rosetta and heart.

Lever espresso machine: lever machines use manual force to drive a piston that generates the pressure required for espresso extraction. Common in the first half of the 20th century, but now largely superseded by electric pump-driven machines.

Long black: a coffee beverage made by adding an espresso on top of hot water. Similar to an Americano, but usually shorter and the crema is preserved.

Macchiato: a coffee beverage consisting of espresso 'stained' with a dash of steamed milk (espresso macchiato) or a tall glass of steamed milk 'stained' with espresso (latte macchiato).

Matcha: Finely ground powder of specially grown and processed green tea. The matcha plants are shade-grown for three weeks before harvest.

Microfoam: the preferred texture of finely-steamed milk for espresso-based coffee drinks. Essential for pouring latte art. Achieved by incorporating a lesser quantity of air during the milk steaming process.

Micro-lot coffee: coffee originating from a small, discrete area within a farm, typically benefiting from conditions favorable to the development of a particular set of characteristics. Micro-lot coffees tend to fetch higher prices due to their unique nature.

Mocha, caffè mocha: similar to a caffè latte, but with added chocolate syrup or powder.

Natural process: a simple method of processing coffee where whole cherries (with the bean inside) are dried on raised beds under the sun. Typically results in a lower acidity coffee with a heavier body and exotic flavors.

Over extracted: describes coffee with a bitter or burnt taste, resulting from ground coffee exposed to hot water for too long.

Peaberry: a small, round coffee bean formed when only one seed, rather than the usual two, develops in a coffee cherry. Peaberry beans produce a different flavor profile, typically lighter-bodied with higher acidy.

Piccolo: a short Italian coffee beverage made with espresso topped with an equal quantity of steamed milk. Traditionally served in a glass.

Pod: a self-contained, pre-ground, pre-pressed puck of coffee, individually wrapped inside a perforated paper filter. Mostly found in domestic espresso machines. Often compatible only with certain equipment brands.

Pour over: a type of drip filter method in which a thin, steady stream of water is poured slowly over a bed of ground coffee contained within a filter cone.

Pouring kettle: a kettle with a narrow swan-neck spout specifically designed to deliver a steady, thin stream of water.

Portafilter: consists of a handle (usually plastic) attached to a metal cradle that holds the filter basket. Inserted into the group head and locked in place in preparation for making an espresso. Usually features a single or double spout on the underside to direct the flow of coffee into a cup.

Portafilter basket: a flat bottomed, bowl-shaped metal insert that sits in the portafilter and holds a bed of ground coffee. The basket has an array of tiny holes in the base allowing extracted coffee to seep through and pour into a cup.

Puck: immediately after an espresso extraction, the bed of spent coffee grounds forms compressed waste matter resembling a small hockey puck.

Pull: the act of pouring an espresso. The term originates from the first half of the 20th century when manual machines were the norm, and baristas pulled a lever to create an espresso.

Ristretto: a shorter 'restricted' shot of espresso. Made using the same dose and brew time as for a regular espresso, but with less water. The result is a richer and more intense beverage.

Roast: the process by which green coffee is heated in order to produce coffee beans ready for consumption. Caramelization occurs as intense heat converts starches in the bean to simple sugars, imbuing the bean with flavor and transforming its color to a golden brown.

Robusta, Coffea canephora: the second most widely cultivated coffee species after arabica, robusta accounts for approximately 30% of the world's coffee. Robusta is hardier and grown at lower altitudes than arabica. It has a much higher caffeine content than arabica, and a less refined flavor. Commonly used in instant coffee blends.

Shot: a single unit of brewed espresso.

Single origin, single estate: coffee from one particular region or farm.

Siphon brewer, vacuum brewer: an unusual brewing method that relies on the action of a vacuum to draw hot water through coffee from one glass chamber to another. The resulting brew is remarkably clean.

Small batch: refers to roasting beans in small quantities, typically between 4-24kg, but sometimes larger.

Speciality coffee: a premium quality coffee scoring 80 points or above (from a total of 100) in the SCAA grading scale.

Steam wand: the protruding pipe found on an espresso machine that supplies hot steam used to froth and steam milk.

Stovetop, moka pot: a brewing method that makes strong coffee (but not espresso). Placed directly on a heat source, hot water is forced by steam pressure from the lower chamber to the upper chamber, passing through a bed of coffee.

Tamp: the process of distributing and pressing ground coffee into a compact bed within the portafilter basket in preparation for brewing espresso. The degree of pressure applied during tamping is a key variable in espresso extraction. Too light and the brew water will percolate rapidly (tending to under extract), too firm and the water flow will be impeded (tending to over extract).

Tamper: the small pestle-like tool used to distribute and compact ground coffee in the filter basket.

Third wave coffee: the movement that treats coffee as an artisanal foodstuff rather than a commodity product. Quality coffee reflects its terroir, in a similar manner to wine.

Under extracted: describes coffee that has not been exposed to brew water for long enough. The resulting brew is often sour and thin-bodied.

V60: a popular type of pour over coffee brewer marketed by Hario. The product takes its name from the 60° angle of the V-shaped cone. Typically used to brew one or two cups only.

Washed process: one of the most common methods of processing coffee cherries. Involves fermentation in tanks of water to remove mucilage. Typically results in a clean and bright flavor profile with higher acidity.

Whole bean: coffee that has been roasted but not ground.

A-Z List of Coffee Venues

A-Z List of Coffee Venues contd.

A-Z List of Coffee Venues contd.

Photo: Tyler Nix